THE REALLY, REALLY
REALLY EASY
STEP-BY-STEP
COMPUTER
BOOK 1 (XP)

for absolute beginners
of all ages

NEW HOLLAND

Contents and progress

TICK THINGS OFF AS YOU LEARN THEM ✔

CHAPTER 1 – GETTING STARTED — 6

Switching on your computer — 6

The 'Desktop' — 8

Telling your computer what to do — 8

Using the mouse — 8

Opening (loading) a program — 9

Filling the whole screen — 13

Minimizing a program's window out of view — 14

Closing (exiting) a program — 15

Shutting down your computer — 16

Logging off and on — 17

CHAPTER 2 – CREATING TYPED DOCUMENTS — 19

Loading Microsoft Office Word — 19

Getting to know the 'Word' window — 22

The Scrollbars — 24

Saving a Word document — 24

Typing a document — 27

Working in different document layout views — 30

Starting a new document — 31

Closing a file — 31

Opening a saved file — 33

Printing a document — 34

Using alternative methods — 35

Typing with different font styles — 37

Using shortcuts to select text — 42

Moving to different places in a document — 44

Copying and moving text — 45

Aligning text — 48

Using bullets or numbers to create itemised lists — 50

Using automatic page numbering — 51

CHAPTER 3 – THE INTERNET — 53

What is the Internet? — 53

Popular uses of the Internet — 54

Three key requirements for Internet access and e-mail — 54

Choosing an Internet package that suits your needs   55
Choosing an Internet service provider   55
Setting up your Internet connection and e-mail settings   56
Creating a dial-up shortcut on your Desktop   56
Connecting to the Internet   57
Disconnecting from the Internet   59

CHAPTER 4 – SURFING THE INTERNET   60
What is the World Wide Web?   60
Connecting to the Internet   60
Opening Internet Explorer   61
Three main approaches to the Web   62
Going to a specific Web site   62
Navigating Web pages   63
Bookmarking a site for future visits   65
Going straight to one of your favourite Web pages   66
Searching the Web for information   67

CHAPTER 5 – E-MAIL   71
What is e-mail?   71
Setting up your e-mail account   71
Opening Outlook Express   72
Writing an e-mail   72
Attaching a file to your e-mail   75
Sending an e-mail   77
Receiving e-mail   78
Disconnecting from the Internet   79
Reading new mail   79
Opening and viewing attached files   81
Deleting e-mails   83
Replying to an e-mail   84
Forwarding an e-mail to someone else   85
Saving an address in the address book   85
Using the address book when creating a new e-mail   88
Sending an e-mail to several recipients at once   89
Finding an e-mail you're looking for   90

CHAPTER 6 – QUICK REFERENCE   91
Useful shortcuts   91

INDEX   93

Read this before you start

RELAX!

Using a computer is not as difficult as you might imagine. In fact it's really, really, really easy when you're led by the hand, step by step, as you will be in this book.

The goal of this book is to get you up and running and using your computer in the shortest possible time, without any frustrating waffle or unnecessary technical jargon along the way. In no time, you'll be:

- typing and printing your own documents;
- accessing the awesome information and entertainment resources that are available on the World Wide Web – often referred to as 'surfing the Net';
- communicating via e-mail with friends, family members or business associates.

| External Modem for Internet | Computer Tower | Monitor/Screen | Keyboard | Mouse on Pad | Printer |

A typical basic computer setup

HOW TO USE THE VISUAL SYSTEM

This book's user-friendly visual system makes it easy for anyone to enjoy learning how to do things on a personal computer.

Colour-coded windows are used throughout the book, so that you can see at a glance the *type* of information you're looking at:

- introductions and explanations in normal black text on a white background;

- step-by-step procedures in yellow boxes;

- hints and tips in blue boxes;

- very important notes and warnings in boxes with red borders;

- special exercises in green boxes.

The detailed step-by-step procedures are well-supported, where necessary, with pictures to clarify what you'll see on your computer screen.

THIS IS A <u>WORKBOOK</u> – DON'T SKIP ANY CHAPTERS!
Each chapter builds on the information provided in earlier chapters, so it's important not to skip chapters or jump around between pages. Treat this manual as a workbook; have it next to you as you use the computer to work your way through each chapter and each topic. The checklist on the preceding Contents and Progress pages will help you to make steady progress and become pretty competent very quickly.

So, let's get started right away.

1 Getting started

SWITCHING ON YOUR COMPUTER

Before you can start working with your computer you'll need to turn its power on if it's not already switched on.

1. Look at the front of the computer (either a '**tower**' box that looks something like the picture below left, or a **laptop** like the picture below right) to check whether the power light is on. If so, the computer is already switched on and you're ready to start.

2. If there are no lights illuminated, look for the **power-on** button and press it in firmly to power-up the computer; you'll hear the cooling fan inside the box start whirring. (Older computers may have an up-down power switch, sometimes on the side of the box. On a laptop, the power-on button will possibly be somewhere near the typing keys, and have a ⏻ 'power' symbol on it.)

Typical Power-On button location on a computer tower

Typical Power-On button location on a laptop computer

EVERY COMPUTER IS DIFFERENT

Newer versions of computer systems and programs are constantly being released, and each individual user has their system set up according to their own preferences or those of the person who set their system up for them. So if what you see on your computer screen differs from what you see in this book, it simply means that your system is set up differently from ours. Generally we've used the standard (or 'default') settings, but there might still be variations, so you may occasionally need to allow for differences and adapt as necessary.

On start-up, depending on how Windows XP was installed, your computer may display the Windows XP Welcome screen showing your user name, and possibly a little text window into which you need to type your password. Some computers have been set up to bypass this step.

If the log-in window pops up, here's how to log in:

3. Click on your **User Name** to select it.
4. If required, **type your password** into the little text window.
5. Press the ⌨ Enter key on your keyboard to activate the log-in process.
6. Wait a minute or so while the computer loads its operating system, in our case Windows XP. (This process is called 'booting up', and is usually accompanied by little flickering lights on the front of the computer.)

Once booting up is completed, the little lights will stop flickering and your monitor's screen should look something like the examples below, although probably not *exactly* the same, because everyone's computer is set up differently.

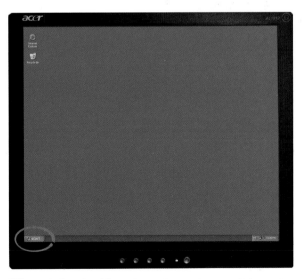

Different computers have different visual settings

THE 'DESKTOP'

The area on the monitor's screen as shown on the previous page is called the **Desktop**. It's something like your real desk's surface, which has some important items on it, while other items are stowed away out of sight. On the computer's Desktop the hidden items can be accessed via the **Start** button at the bottom left-hand corner of the screen (see red circles on the previous page). You'll be doing this shortly.

TELLING YOUR COMPUTER WHAT TO DO

The 'software' that operates the computer is called the Operating System ('OS'). This book is based on the Microsoft Windows XP Operating System, of which there are two main editions: the Home Edition and the Professional Edition (the edition we've used in this book). The two editions are similar, with the Professional Edition having a few more bells and whistles added to it.

The Operating System gets its instructions from you, the computer operator. You'll be using two pieces of equipment ('hardware') to tell the Windows XP Operating System what you want it to do. These are the **mouse** and the **keyboard** (which is the modern electronic version of the keyboard found on the old-fashioned typewriter).

USING THE MOUSE

The mouse is used to activate digital images on the computer screen. Many of the modern mouse models communicate with the computer using wireless signals, while others are connected to the computer by means of a thin cable.

Here's how to use the mouse to point to items on the screen's Desktop.

Moving the mouse
to point to items

1. Place the heel of your hand on the desk in front of the mouse.
2. Hold the mouse between your thumb and ring fingers.
3. Place your index finger on the left mouse button.
4. With your wrist resting lightly on the desk, move the whole mouse in a small circle on its mat (called a **mouse pad**), and watch the screen while you do this.
5. Look for the little arrow-shaped **pointer** on the screen and see how it moves around to follow the movements you make with the mouse.
6. Now move the mouse straight to the left, then to the right, then away from you, and lastly towards you, and notice the corresponding movements of the pointer on the screen.

Clicking the mouse buttons to activate items

Once you point to something on the screen and have the pointer hovering over the item, you now need to give the computer its instruction on what to do with that item. This is done by pressing one of the mouse buttons (called *clicking*) as explained below:

Pointing means moving the mouse so that the pointer touches the object on the screen that you wish to select or activate.

Clicking means depressing the left-hand mouse button **once** and releasing it. This is the most common form of clicking used, and it is usually done to activate a particular item displayed on the screen.

Double-clicking means depressing the left mouse button **twice** in quick succession. This is usually done to open a program, folder or file, which you'll do in the next topic.

Right-clicking means pressing the mouse button on the right side of the mouse once and releasing it. This opens a menu of options.

TIP: THE MIDDLE BUTTON OR WHEEL

Most mouse models these days also have a button or a wheel between the left and right buttons. This is usually pressed (or rolled) forward or backward to scroll up or down on the page you're viewing on the screen. Another useful tip to know is that if your mouse has a wheel between the two main buttons, you can hold down the Ctrl **Control** key on your keyboard and move the wheel forwards to magnify the content on the page or backwards to decrease the size of the page content. You can experiment with the centre wheel/button options later.

OPENING (LOADING) A PROGRAM

To make use of your computer you'll need to use some 'software', which is commonly referred to as a **program** or **application**. Different programs are used for different purposes, like typing documents, viewing pictures, listening to music and so on. The program we'll be using to create a text document in the next chapter is called **Microsoft Office Word** (also referred to as **MS Word** or just **Word**). We're going to use the mouse to open that program now.

1. With the Desktop showing on your screen, move the mouse so that the ↖ pointer is on the **start** button in the bottom left-hand corner of the screen, and click on that button (depress the left mouse button) to open the **Start Menu** (see illustration below).

2. Next, click on **All Programs**, just above the **Start** button (see next illustration).
3. When the next layer of the menu pops up (called a sub-menu) displaying all the programs on your computer, move your pointer over (or click on) **Microsoft Office** to open the next sub-menu showing the programs in the Microsoft Office group.
4. Finally, click on **Microsoft Office Word 2003** (you may have a different version/ name of MS Word), and wait while Windows XP loads the Word application onto the Desktop.

TIP: NO MICROSOFT 'OFFICE'?

If you don't see **Microsoft Office** in the menu list, but only **Microsoft Word**, this suggests that you have **Word** installed on its own and not as part of the Microsoft Office suite of four programs. That's fine. Simply click on **Microsoft Word** as in Step 4 above.

TIP: NO MICROSOFT 'WORD'?

If you don't see **Microsoft Word** anywhere in the menu list, this suggests that you don't have **Word** installed on your computer at all. No need to panic; you can use Word's little brother **Microsoft WordPad** instead. **WordPad** comes with Windows XP, so you should definitely have it. Click on **Start**, then on **All Programs**, then on **Accessories**. Look in the list for **WordPad,** then click on it to open the program.

IF YOU'RE USING WORDPAD INSTEAD OF WORD

WordPad is a very basic or 'light' version of Microsoft Word. The next chapter is based on Microsoft Word, not WordPad. If you don't have Word installed on your computer, you'll need to adapt accordingly when you look at the illustrations of the screen shots as well as some of the procedures. But don't be concerned – nearly all the topics covered in Chapter 2 *can* be done with either WordPad or Word. It's just that many people prefer using Word, and so we've chosen that program for the tutorials. The illustrations of the screen shots will therefore be a little different from those one would see when using WordPad.

Once Word or WordPad has fully loaded, your screen should look like this:

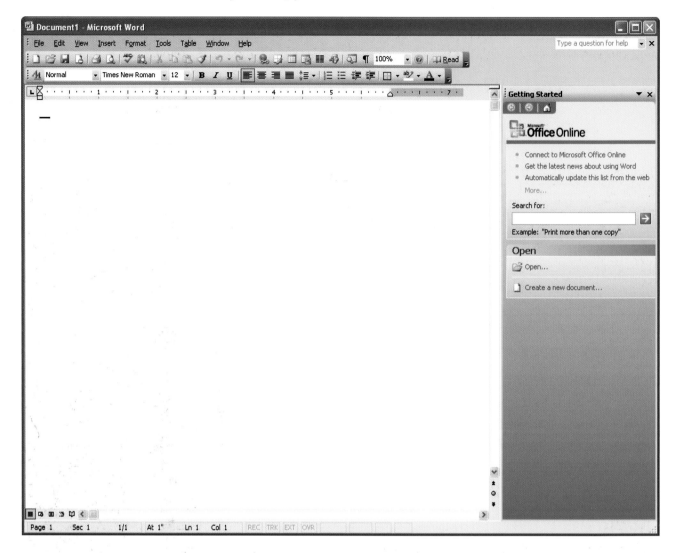

Microsoft Word screen

WordPad has fewer options on its Menu Bar and Toolbars at the top of the window compared with Word.

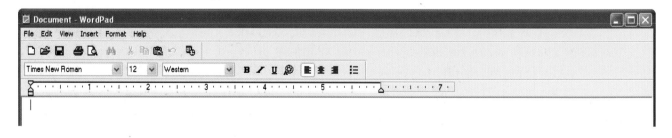

WordPad screen

FILLING THE WHOLE SCREEN

Sometimes when a program is loaded it doesn't fill the whole screen. This just means the program's window is not **maximized**. If this happens, you can easily change it as follows:

1. Note the three little buttons in the top right-hand corner of the program's window.

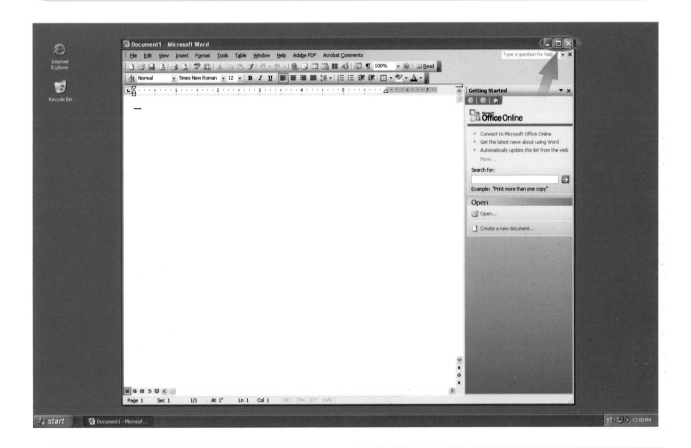

2. Move your mouse so that the pointer rests on the middle button and hold it there – the one with the bold line at the top of the little square.
3. Click on that middle ▢ **Maximize** button. The program window will fill the entire screen, and the button's icon will change.

TIP: USE THE 'TOOLTIPS'
Note that after pointing at a button for one or two seconds, a little **ToolTip** box pops up with some text in it to tell you what the button is for. (Remember this useful little Windows XP feature.)

MINIMIZING A PROGRAM'S WINDOW OUT OF VIEW

Sometimes you'll need to clear the program window temporarily from view without closing (exiting) the program altogether – perhaps to work briefly in a different program or to see your Desktop. To do this, you simply **minimize** the program as follows:

1.   Move the mouse pointer to the three buttons in the top right-hand corner of the program.
2.   Click on the left ▬ **Minimize** button with the little line at the bottom and the program will disappear from view.

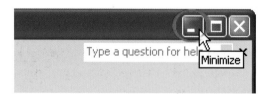

The Minimize button is available in all programs

3.   Look down at the **Taskbar** (the blue strip near the bottom edge of the screen) and you'll see the **Word** icon there with the name of your document next to it. This **task button** indicates that the Word program is still loaded, but just not open for view on the screen.

Task button on the Taskbar showing the open program/file

4. Click on that **Word** task button on the Taskbar and the program will be restored to its previous view mode again.

CLOSING (EXITING) A PROGRAM

If you want to work in a different program for a while, and no longer need to work in the program you have open, it's a good idea to close the unused program completely. This frees up some of the computer's *memory,* so that the computer's functioning doesn't slow down unnecessarily due to several programs being loaded and running at the same time. Here's how to close a program:

1. Click on the red **Close** button in the top right-hand corner of the open program's window, and the program will close down and disappear from view altogether (there will be no task button on the Taskbar).
2. If a message pops up asking whether you want to save the changes, click on the appropriate button, **Yes** or **No.** (Saving changes is covered in Chapter 2.)
3. Repeat this for any other programs that are still open; when all programs have been closed you'll be back at the Desktop again.

> **!**
> **CLOSE ALL PROGRAMS BEFORE SHUTTING DOWN YOUR COMPUTER**
> You should *always* close all open programs before switching off the computer. The more programs you have running, the longer it takes Windows to close each one before shutting itself down. (If you have unsaved work, you should save this before closing a program. Chapter 2 explains how to save files.)

SHUTTING DOWN YOUR COMPUTER

To switch off a computer, it is important to follow the correct procedure:

1. Click on the  **start** button in the bottom left-hand corner of the screen.
2. In the Start Menu that opens, click on the red ⓞ **Turn Off Computer** button.

All Programs ▶

Run...

Log Off   Turn Off Computer

start

3. Lastly, in the next little window that comes up in the centre of the screen, click on the red **Turn Off** button (see illustration on the right), and wait for your computer to complete the shutting-down process. (This may take a minute or so.)

This procedure is important because it gives the computer the opportunity to save your settings.

 DON'T JUST SWITCH OFF THE POWER
Under normal circumstances never switch off the computer's power without first following the proper *Turn Off Computer* procedure just described. However, if your computer should stop responding (this is called 'freezing'), and simply won't allow you to turn it off using the correct procedure, then you may have no option but to switch it off with the power supply switch. If you do have to turn off the power with the power switch, the next time you turn your computer on it will run a *Disk Scan* to check for errors that may have occurred because the computer power was abnormally interrupted. This also occurs if there has been a power failure.

TIP: TURNING OFF AND RESTARTING

Repeatedly turning a computer off and on increases wear and tear, more so than simply leaving it on. So if you intend using your computer intermittently during the day, it's best to leave it switched on until you shut down at the end of your working day. But it's a good idea to turn off the monitor if it will be idle for half an hour or more, to save power and prolong the monitor's life.

If you're using several programs at once for quite a while, or using programs that use up a lot of resources, you may find the computer gets a bit sluggish after a time. If this happens, you can go through the **Start**, **Turn Off Computer** process already described, but in the final step click on **Restart** instead of **Turn Off**. Restarting a computer is also referred to as **Rebooting**.

LOGGING OFF AND ON

If you'll be leaving your computer unattended for a while, or if there is someone else who wishes to use it, you can use the **Switch User** or the **Log Off** options explained below:

1. Click on the **start** button in the bottom left-hand corner of the screen.
2. Click on the orange **Log Off** button to open the next window showing the Switch User and Log Off options.

3. Decide what you want the computer to do (see the explanations underneath each screenshot below) and click on either the **Switch User** or the **Log Off** button accordingly.

Log Off option

Switch User option

- Click on **Log Off** when you want to shut down all open programs and stop working for some time, but leave the computer running.
- This option saves your work, shuts down all open programs and returns you to the Welcome screen for you or any other user to log on again.
- If your User Name is password-protected, no one else will be able to access your files once you've logged off.

- Click on **Switch User** when someone else needs to use the computer, after which you want to return to whatever you were working on.
- When the other person is finished, click on **Start**, **Log Off**, **Switch User**, and then log back on and everything will be as you left it with your programs and files still open.
- If your User Name is password-protected you will have to re-enter your password to log on again.

NOTE: SWITCH USER OPTION
The **Switch User** option is available only when
two or more user accounts have been set up.

2 Creating typed documents

In this chapter you'll learn how to create, format and print documents such as letters, reports and the like. To do this, you'll be using the program called **Microsoft Office Word** (Word, for short) that you opened and closed in Chapter 1.

REMEMBER: NO 'MICROSOFT OFFICE WORD'?

If you don't have Word installed, then use WordPad, as explained in Chapter 1. You'll then need to adapt as necessary as you follow the procedures and screenshots in this chapter.

LOADING MICROSOFT OFFICE WORD

1. Look on the Desktop, and if there's a shortcut to Word (like the icon shown here on the right), double-click on it to load Microsoft Office Word. (The little curved black arrow on the bottom left of the icon indicates that it is a shortcut.)

If there's no such shortcut icon, continue with Steps 2 to 5 below.

2. Using the mouse, click on **start** (bottom left-hand corner of the screen), point to **All Programs**, then **Microsoft Office**, and in the sub-menu that opens position the pointer over **Microsoft Office Word**.

3. **Right**-click on **Microsoft Office Word** to open a sub-menu.

4. Point to **Send To**, so that the menu expands further, then click on **Desktop (create shortcut)** and Windows will place the shortcut icon on your Desktop.

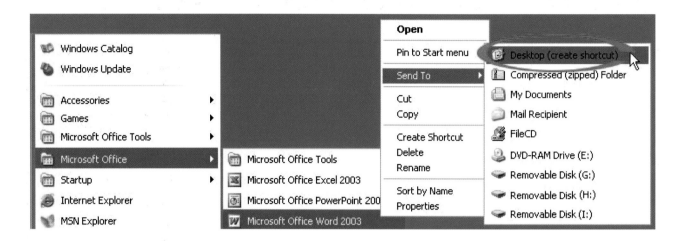

5. On the Desktop, **double**-click on that shortcut icon to load Word.

NOTE: THE PROGRAM'S NAME

Depending on which version of Word or Microsoft Office is installed on your computer, the program may be called Microsoft Word, or Microsoft Office Word 2003, or some similar name.

Once Word has loaded, your screen should show the Word window like this:

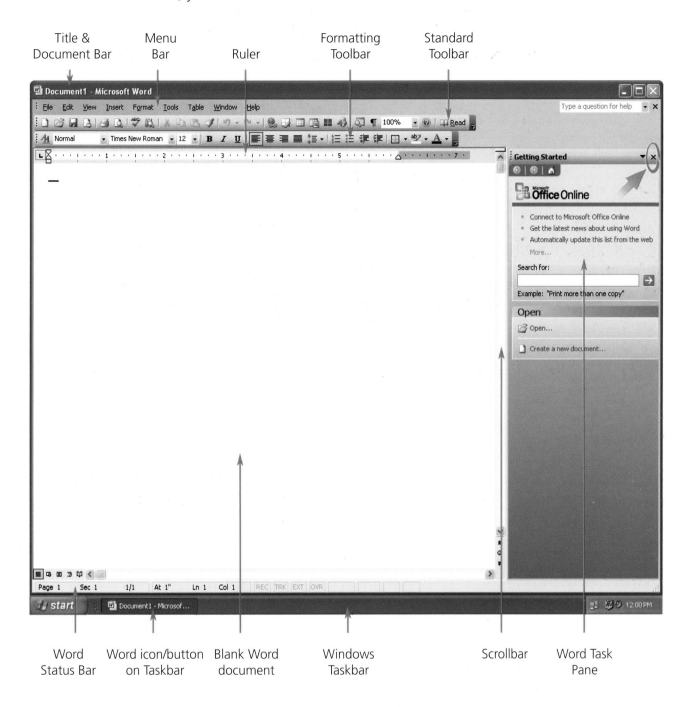

Title & Document Bar   Menu Bar   Ruler   Formatting Toolbar   Standard Toolbar

Word Status Bar   Word icon/button on Taskbar   Blank Word document   Windows Taskbar   Scrollbar   Word Task Pane

Note the **Task Pane** on the right-hand side of the Word window. You can explore that later, but for now let's close it as follows:

1. In the Task Pane on the right, use the left mouse button to click once on the little ✕ **Close** button next to the words **Getting Started**; this will close the Task Pane.

> **TIP: ALWAYS CLICK ON THE APPLICABLE 'X' BUTTON**
>
> Notice that in the previous screenshot there are, in fact, three items open:
>
> (1) the Microsoft Office Word program; (2) a new blank document ready for typing; and
>
> (3) the Task Pane. Each of these has its own **X** for closing that particular window.
>
> When closing an item, always make sure you're about to click on the applicable **X**
>
> or you could end up closing the whole program instead of just the document,
>
> or closing the document instead of the Task Pane.

GETTING TO KNOW THE 'WORD' WINDOW

The coloured Title and Document Bar

Active (dark blue) Title Bar

When a window is active (can be worked with), the **Title and Document Bar** at the very top of the window is darkened (see illustration above) and the window will respond to your keyboard commands. When it's inactive the bar will be a lighter shade (see below).

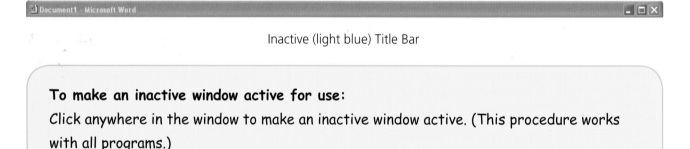

Inactive (light blue) Title Bar

> **To make an inactive window active for use:**
> Click anywhere in the window to make an inactive window active. (This procedure works with all programs.)

The Menu Bar

Menu Bar

Each heading on the Menu Bar opens a door to a menu of items, each of which can be selected by clicking on it (provided the menu item's text is black and not grey). If it's 'greyed-out', this means that particular option is not available for the situation you're working with.

1. Click on any menu heading to view its menu list.
2. Where you see ▶ on the right of a menu item, move the mouse pointer onto that item to see an expanded sub-menu. (There may be a very brief delay of a second or two before the sub-menu appears.)

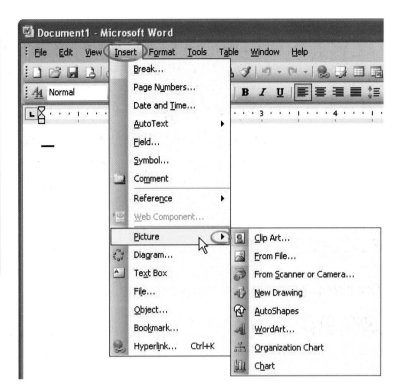

Menu expanded to show sub-menu

TIP: SHORTENED MENUS

If the drop-down menu shows a 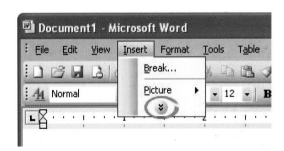 button at the bottom with two down-arrows on it, this means that Word will display the full menu after a short delay of several seconds.
To view the full list of menu options sooner, simply click on that double-arrow button.

Double-arrow button indicates more menu items available

The Toolbars

Standard Toolbar with Formatting Toolbar below it

The buttons (icons) on a Toolbar act as a quick way for you to give the computer a command, such as opening a new blank document or a saved document, printing a document, copying selected text, and so on. To activate a button you simply click on it once.

TIP: MENUS OFFER MORE OPTIONS THAN TOOLBAR BUTTONS

THE SCROLLBARS

The Scrollbars are used to move through a document. This is explained in more detail on page 44.

SAVING A WORD DOCUMENT

You can store your work on your computer for future reference or for subsequent editing or printing. We call this **saving** the document as a **file**.

NOTE: THE WINDOWS FILING SYSTEM

Windows has a computerized equivalent of an office filing cabinet that has drawers, sections, folders and documents. In Windows your documents, photos, and so on are called **files**. These files can then be stored away in **folders**. Within any folder you can have **sub-folders,** which are simply folders stored within folders – something like folders stored within a section of a filing cabinet drawer.

 SAVE BEFORE WORKING IN A DOCUMENT
When you start a new document it's always a good idea to give the new document a file name immediately and to save it before you start working in it. From then on you can do a quick-save regularly, as will be explained in this section.

Here's how to save a Word document:

1. Make sure **Word** is still open with a blank document on your screen.
2. On the **Menu Bar** at the top of the Word window, click on <u>**File**</u>, then on <u>**Save**</u>, and a **Save As** dialog box will open and ask you where you want the file stored, and what name you want to give the file.

By default, the **Save As** dialog box offers to save the file in a folder called **My Documents**, with a document number as the **file name**. If **My Documents** does not show in the **Save in** window in your version of Word:

3. Click on the little ⌄ **Down** arrow, find **My Documents** in the list that is displayed and double-click on it to select **My Documents** as the destination folder.

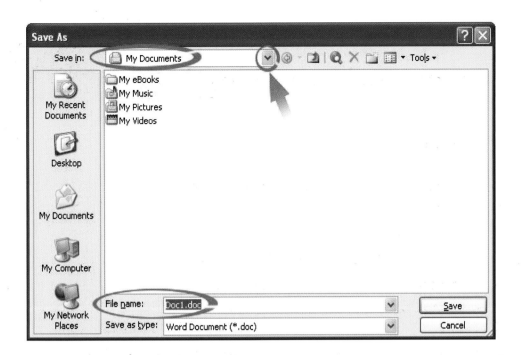

Let's accept the folder **My Documents** as being where we want the file stored for now. As you're going to be using the document to practice some typing, let's give the document a meaningful name, like **Typing**. The suggested file name shown in the **File name:** window has already been selected by Word (highlighted in blue), so it's ready for you to start typing your new file name straight into that window.

4. **Without clicking anywhere**, type the word **Typing**, and Word will immediately over-write the suggested name with your new file name **Typing**. (If the suggested file name is not highlighted in blue, click in the window just behind the name, then press and hold down the Backspace key to erase the document name offered by Word so that the **File name:** window is blank, then type your new file name into that little window.)

TIP: USE MEANINGFUL FILE NAMES

It's useful to give a file a meaningful (and preferably fairly short) name
so that you can easily identify what you're looking for at a later date.

5. In the little **Save as type:** window at the bottom of the dialog box, check that the file type is shown as **.doc**. If it isn't, click on the little ⌄ **Down** arrow on the right of it to find and click on the **Word Document (*.doc)** option in order to select it.

6. Click on the **Save** button near the right-hand bottom of the dialog box.

That's it. You've just saved your first Word document and you're ready to start typing in it.

To help you quickly identify which file you're currently working with, Word updates the Title and Document Bar at the top left of the Word window to show the document's new file name; in this case it changed it from **Document 1** to **Typing**.

Saving new changes to a saved document

Once a document has been saved, you can continue typing and editing it, and save it again to store your new updates. When you do this, Word automatically replaces the earlier version with the updated one and retains the file name you gave it when you first saved it; it does this in the background without opening the **Save As** dialog box every time.

If you forget to save your latest changes when you decide to close the document or the Word program, Word will remind you and ask you if you want to save your changes first. Click on **Yes** to save the changes.

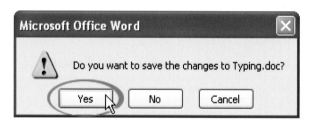

TIP: A QUICK WAY TO SAVE A FILE

Use the keyboard shortcut method: hold down the `Ctrl` key and tap the `S` key once. Windows will save your file in the background. You can continue typing immediately. If you use this method and make frequent saving a permanent habit, you'll never be frustrated by losing a lot of unsaved work if there's a power failure. Try it now and see how easy it is: `Ctrl` + `S` .

You can also use this shortcut with a new document you're saving for the first time.

In this case, Word will open the **Save As** dialog box to let you give the new file a name.

Thereafter the dialog box won't pop up every time you press `Ctrl` + `S` .

Word will simply do the usual background save.

SAVE FREQUENTLY
It can be extremely frustrating to do a lot of typing and formatting and then lose all the new unsaved work you've done because of a power failure or some other problem with your computer. And the more work you've done and not saved, the bigger the crisis can be. So make a habit of saving very often, like every few minutes or after every paragraph you've typed.

TYPING A DOCUMENT

If you've never typed before, here's your opportunity to become an instant two-finger typist. With Word still open and the new blank, saved document on the screen, you'll notice that there is a thin black vertical line flashing near the top left of the blank white page. This shows you where the **cursor** is positioned – in other words, where characters will start appearing on the page when you press the keys on the keyboard. Let's start right now.

Typing words

1. Press the keyboard letters to type your first name (don't bother about capitals just yet).
2. Press the long ⌷ Spacebar ⌷ key – which may or may not have the word **Spacebar** printed on it – at the bottom of the keyboard to add a space after your first name. (You'll see the cursor jump forward one space.)
3. Type your surname.
4. Press the Backspace key several times and see how each letter is deleted with each pressing of the Backspace key.

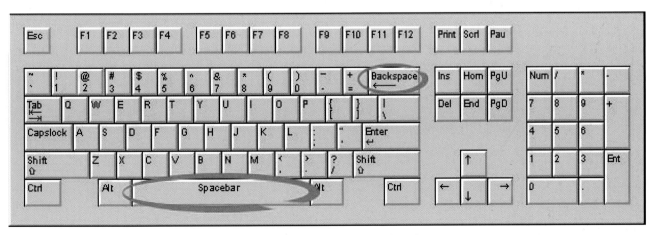

A typical computer keyboard

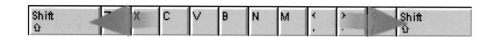

Typing with capital letters

There are two ways to type capital letters (or type in **upper case** as it's called). Try them now.

To type just one capital letter:

1. Hold down either of the [Shift ⇧] **Shift** keys (typically by using the little finger of your left hand to hold down the left shift key) and tap the letter you wish to type, and it will appear in upper case.

To type a word or sentence in upper case:

1. Press and release the [Capslock] key on the keyboard to lock the upper case, and type the word or sentence.
2. Press and release the [Capslock] key again to unlock the upper case and revert to lower case typing.

Using keys that have two characters on them

Some keyboard keys have two characters on them, one above the other, for example:

          `!`   `&`   `%`   `?`   `:`   `"`
          `1`   `7`   `5`   `/`   `;`   `'`

To type the lower character on a key:
Simply press the applicable key as you're typing. Try it now.

To type the upper character on a key:
Hold down the ⇧ Shift key and press the applicable key – e.g. ⇧ Shift + `?⁄` = ?
Try it now.

Typing sentences and paragraphs

When you type a sentence that is longer than the width of the Word page, Word automatically 'wraps' the text to continue on the next line without your having to do anything to make this happen. So when you type long sentences there's nothing you need to do besides continue typing and pressing the Spacebar after each word and after the full stop (or 'period') to create a character space.

TYPING EXERCISE 2:

1. **Type this:** I am so happy I have started to use a computer.
2. **Press** [Enter↵] to move down one line.
3. **Type this:** I ALSO LOVE TO TYPE HEADINGS IN UPPER CASE. If I were to write a test based on this work, I would aim for 100%. And as I type this longer sentence I notice how Word simply wraps the text over onto the next line, automatically, as I keep typing. I wonder how it knows how to do that? Wow! This is great! I'm really having fun!
4. **Press** [Enter↵] **twice** to move down two lines.
5. **Type this:** Using a computer is much easier than I expected. And after pressing Enter twice I now notice that there is a space between the paragraph above and this new paragraph I am typing now.
6. **Press** [Enter↵] **twice** to move down two lines again.
7. **Type this:** Okay, I think I'm getting the hang of this now. I'll practise typing some more as I work through this book page by page.

When you've completed the exercise your typed work should look like this:

```
I am so happy I have started to use a computer.
I ALSO LOVE TO TYPE HEADINGS IN UPPER CASE. If I were to write a
test based on this work, I would aim for 100%. And as I type this
longer sentence I notice how Word simply wraps the text over onto
the next line, automatically, as I keep typing. Wow! This is great!
I'm really having fun!

Using a computer is much easier than I expected. And after pressing
Enter twice, I now notice that there is a space between the
paragraph above and this new paragraph I am typing now.

Okay, I think I am getting the hang of this now. I'll practise
typing some more as I work through this book page by page.
```

TIP: INDENTING WITH THE TAB KEY

Another way to show the start of a new paragraph, without creating a blank line space,
is to indent the first line of the new paragraph by pressing the **Tab** key.

WORKING IN DIFFERENT DOCUMENT LAYOUT VIEWS

There are two popular document viewing options when you're working in a document:

Normal View This is the basic view for typing, editing and formatting text quickly. It does not show page boundaries, headers, footers, images, and so on.

Print Layout View This is the best option for viewing your document with all its elements – headers, footers, margins, columns, images – as they would appear when the page is printed.

To the left of the bottom Scrollbar in the Word window, click on the **View** button of your choice. Try each one now to see how it works.

STARTING A NEW DOCUMENT

You can start a completely new document even while the other one is still open in the Word window.

1. On the Word Toolbar, click on the ⬜ **New Blank Document** button (usually located on the far left of the Toolbar), and a fresh blank document will open in the Word window on top of the one you were working in.
2. Press `Ctrl` + `S` to save it, and the **Save As** dialog box will open.
3. In the little **File _name:_** window near the bottom of the dialog box type the words:
   `New Document`
4. Click on the **_Save_** button on the dialog box, and the new document will be saved into My Documents with the file name `New Document`, ready for typing.

TIP: NEW DOCUMENT KEYBOARD SHORTCUT

To open a new document you can also simply press
`Ctrl` + `N` (hold down the `Ctrl` key and tap the `N` key once).

NOTE: USING THE MENU BAR METHOD

If you click on **File ▶ New** on the Menu Bar, the Task Pane will open on the right
and offer some alternatives. To start a new blank document, you would need to click
on the **New Blank Document** option in that Task Pane.
The Toolbar and keyboard shortcut methods described above are quicker and easier.

CLOSING A FILE

When you no longer need to work with a document, it's best to close it completely to free up some computer memory as well as to avoid having a cluttered Desktop. Page 15 showed the usual method of clicking on the little **X** in the top right-hand corner of the window you wish to close.

Here's the Menu Bar method for closing a file:

1. On the Menu Bar at the top of the Word window, click on **File**, and a menu will open.
2. In that menu click on **Close**.

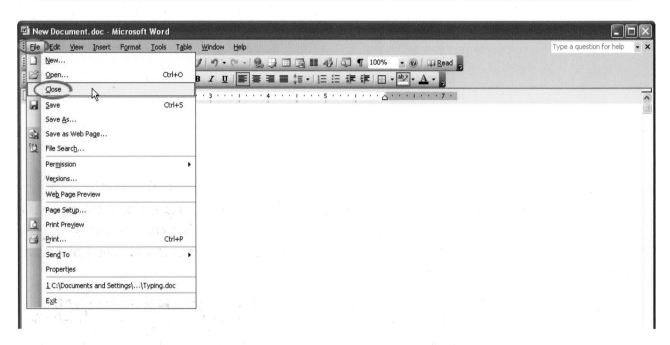

Word will immediately close the document and store it in the My Documents folder, and the other document you previously had open will be visible again in the Word window.

NOTE: KEYBOARD SHORTCUT TO CLOSE ANY WINDOW

Press Alt + F4 and the active window (or program) will close.

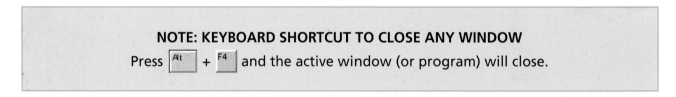

3. Now repeat steps 1 and 2 above to close the second document too, and return to a blank grey Word window with no documents open. (In some set-ups the Word program itself closes when you close the last open document. If this happens, reload Word onto the Desktop to continue with the next topic.)

OPENING A SAVED FILE

1. On the Word **Menu Bar**, click on **File**, then on **Open...** .

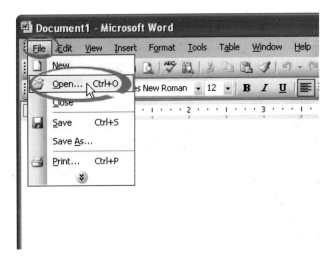

The **Open** dialog box will appear on the screen showing any Word document files that are currently saved in the folder displayed in the **Look in:** window. If **My Documents** is not showing in the **Look in:** window, click the ⌄ down arrow to the right of that little window and browse to **My Documents** and double-click on it in order to see the two documents you saved previously (**Typing.doc** and **New Document.doc**).

2. Click on the file you want to open in order to select it. (It will now be highlighted in blue.)

3. Click on **Open** (on the bottom right of the dialog box) and the selected file will open in the Word window.

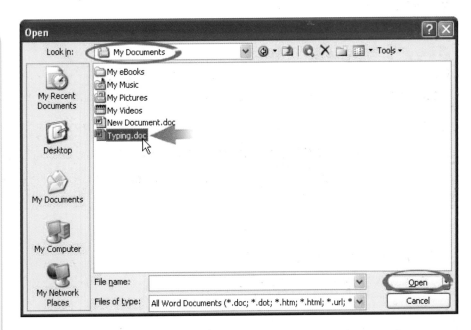

TIP: DOUBLE-CLICK TO OPEN A FILE

A popular way to open a file, instead of clicking on the file name and then on **Open**, is to simply **double**-click on the file name.

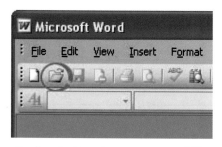

Toolbar button to open a saved file

PRINTING A DOCUMENT

If you have a printer connected to your computer, make sure it's plugged in and switched on, that
there is paper in the tray and that the paper feeder is set up properly.

1. On the **Menu Bar**, click on
   File, then on **Print...** to
   open the **Print** dialog box.

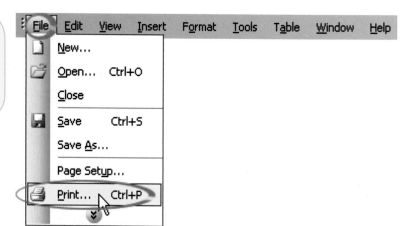

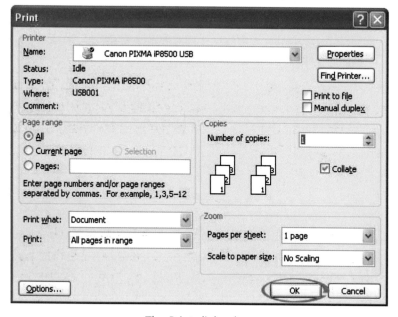

The Print dialog box

2. Click on **OK** and one copy of the document will be printed at the default setting.

TIP: SHORTCUTS FOR PRINTING

A quick way to access the Print dialog box is simply to press `Ctrl` + `P` on the keyboard. You can also click on the 🖨 **Print** icon on the Standard Toolbar. However, note that using the Toolbar icon will simply print one copy of the document at the printer's current default settings and will not open the Print dialog box which allows you to select different settings (e.g. number of copies, print only selected pages, print quality). This is why we said earlier that the Menu Bar offers more options than the Toolbars. (Keyboard shortcuts offer the same options as the Menu Bar.)

USING ALTERNATIVE METHODS

Now that you've learnt a few shortcuts, this is a good time to touch on this topic. With the Windows XP operating system and the various Microsoft applications, there are often several alternative ways to achieve the same goal. Some are slicker and quicker than others. The main options are:

The Menu Bar method

This is often considered to be the 'long way round', and people with less patience usually prefer to use one or other of the shortcut options. Yet for beginners it can be the 'safe way round'.

The Keyboard shortcut method

These shortcuts usually involve holding down one key (like the `Ctrl` **Control** key) while tapping another key, as you've already seen with saving, opening a new document and printing. This method is often quicker than clicking on Menu items, and by doing it often it will become second nature.

The Toolbar shortcut method

Clicking on the applicable Toolbar icon is also a very popular shortcut method, but in some situations it offers fewer options than the first two methods mentioned above. Yet it can be an extremely useful and quick way of doing things.

Pressing 'Enter' (or 'Return') instead of clicking on a button

In a dialog box there is usually one button that is highlighted with a blue shadow around it. (See screenshot – the **OK** button has a blue shadow around it to make it look 'raised'.) This is the button that the program has automatically assumed to be the one you will want to activate next. To activate it you can either click on it as you've done up till now, or you can simply press **Enter** on your keyboard, which is often a much faster option.

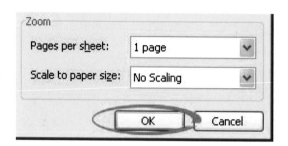

If you want to activate a different option – i.e. the **Cancel** button in the given example – then you need to use the mouse to **click** on that other button. So, remember: if you press **Enter** on your keyboard, the button with the blue shadow around it will be the one that gets activated.

ALWAYS READ THE DIALOG BOX FIRST
Always read the information in a dialog box before clicking with the mouse or pressing [Enter ↵]. This can save you much heartache by preventing you from hastily executing the wrong action.

As you gain experience, you'll start to get a feel of what works best for you in different situations. This sometimes ends up being a variety of methods, where you might use the Menu Bar for some actions, the Toolbars for others, the keyboard shortcuts for yet other actions, and pressing Enter in other situations.

In the next section you'll learn some slightly more advanced features you can use in Microsoft Word to make document-writing easier.

ADDITIONAL USEFUL THINGS YOU CAN DO IN WORD

Word is a very intelligent program and there's almost no end to what you can do with it. Here are some of the more popular functions that Word offers, which even an absolute beginner would find useful.

TYPING WITH DIFFERENT FONT STYLES

Changing the font type and size

The quickest way to change to a different font in your document is to use the Formatting Toolbar's **Font** and **Font Size** selection arrows.

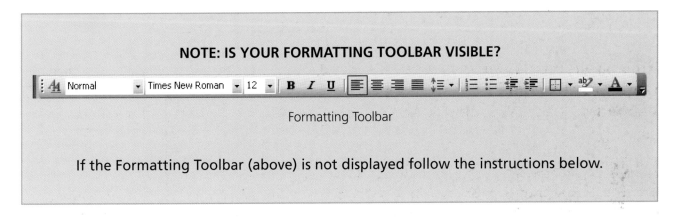

NOTE: IS YOUR FORMATTING TOOLBAR VISIBLE?

Formatting Toolbar

If the Formatting Toolbar (above) is not displayed follow the instructions below.

Displaying toolbars

1. **Right**-click on any blank space below the top Title and Document bar (see below) to open up a list of options.

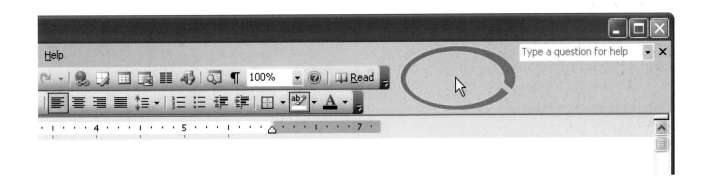

2. In the drop-down menu that opens (see right) click on **Formatting** and the Formatting Toolbar will now appear below the Standard Toolbar.

3. Note the other options in the list that you can investigate at your leisure. (To unselect any item you click on, simply follow steps 1 and 2 above and click on that item again.)

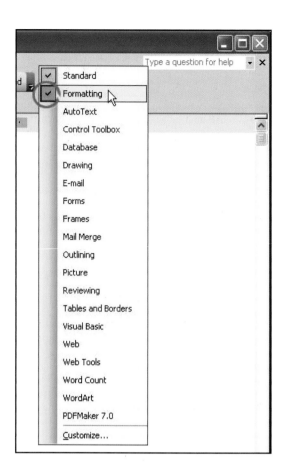

Changing the font type

1. On the **Formatting Toolbar** click on the ▾ **drop-down arrow** just to the right of the **Font** window to open the menu of font type options.

2. In that menu, click on the ⌄ **Scroll Down** button at the bottom right of the menu to see all of the available fonts installed in your computer.

3. Click on the new font you require in order to select it, and the menu will close.

Font Type Menu

Anything you now type in your current document will be in that chosen font type until you change it again.

Changing the font size

1. On the **Formatting Toolbar** click on the next little ▾ **drop-down arrow** just to the right of the **Font Size** window.
2. Click on the new font size you require in order to select it, and the menu will close.

Anything you now type in your current document will be in that chosen font size until you change it again.

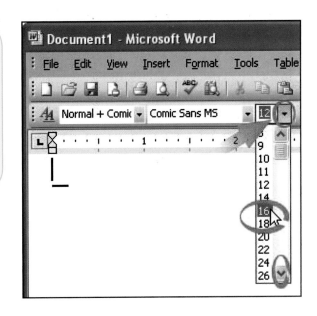

Font Size Menu

Typing in bold font

1. On the **Formatting Toolbar** click on the **B** **Bold** button and continue typing. (Note how the button changes colour and now has a border. Anything you now type in the current document will be **bold** until you change it again.)
2. To change back to normal font click on the **B** **Bold** button again and continue typing. (The button's colour returns to the Toolbar's colour and its border disappears.)

Typing in italics or underlined text

1. Follow the same procedure as for typing in **Bold**, but click on the *I* **Italic** button for **Italics** or on the **U** **Underline** button for **underlined text**. (Anything you now type in your current document will be in italics or underlined until you change it again.)

TIP: KEYBOARD SHORTCUTS FOR FONT FORMATS

A much quicker method is often to use one of the following keyboard shortcuts:

Bold: Ctrl + B   **Italics:** Ctrl + *I*   **Underline:** Ctrl + **U**

To revert to normal font again, just repeat the keyboard shortcut.

Changing the font colour

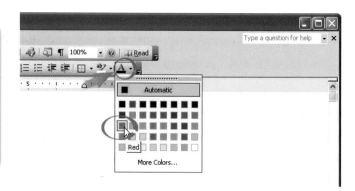

1. On the **Formatting Toolbar** click on the little ▾ drop-down arrow next to the ![A] ▾ **Font Color** icon to open the colour palette.
2. Click on the colour you require, and continue typing.

Anything you now type in your current document will be in the font colour you selected until you change it again.

Changing the font 'default' for all future documents

If you want to change the font so that it is the same on all documents you will be typing in future (until you decide to change the default again), you can set the **default** to the font of your choice.

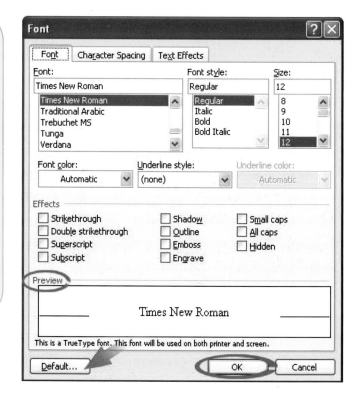

1. On the Menu Bar, click on **Format**, then on **Font...** to open the **Font** dialog box.
2. Select the various font options you require.
3. Instead of clicking on the **OK** button, click on the **Default...** button at the bottom left of the dialog box.
4. In the confirmation dialog box that opens (see next page), click on **Yes**.

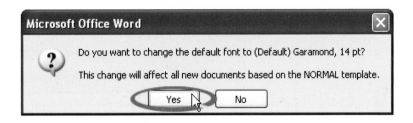

All new documents that you create from now on will open with those new **default** settings. To change the defaults again, follow the same procedure.

Changing the font of text that's already been typed

You may decide to change the font style of what you've already typed. Here's how:

1. Move the mouse so that the cursor is just before the text you wish to change.
2. Click and hold down the mouse button and carefully move the mouse to the right to **drag** the cursor over the text you want to change, and it will be selected (highlighted) in black like this. Release the mouse button.
3. Press `Ctrl` + `B` to change all of the selected text to **Bold** (for example).
4. Click anywhere else to de-select the highlighted text.
5. To change existing text to *italics* or <u>underlined</u>, select the text as in steps 1 and 2 above and use the appropriate method (see page 39) to change the font.

NOTE: MULTIPLE FORMATS FOR THE SAME TEXT

It's not an 'either/or' situation with font styles. You can have **bold**, or **<u>bold underlined</u>**, or ***<u>bold underlined and italics</u>*** – or any combination of font styles or colours for the same text – by following the methods already explained. Just make sure that the text you want to change is already selected, then use one of the methods to select the font formats and colours you desire.

REMEMBER: YOU CAN EASILY REVERSE TEXT REFORMATTING

To change reformatted text back to its original font, while the text is still selected (i.e. **before** clicking elsewhere) simply click on the appropriate formatting button again, or repeat the keyboard shortcut, or unselect the options selected by using the Menu Bar. To revert to your **default** font at any time, press

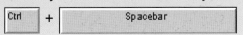

USING SHORTCUTS TO SELECT TEXT

Selecting a single word

1. If necessary, use the Scrollbar on the right of your Word document to get to the text you've already typed (see page 44).
2. Place the cursor over the word you wish to select.
3. Double-click (click twice in quick succession) on that word and it will be selected and highlighted like this .
4. To de-select it, click once anywhere in the document.

Selecting a full line of text

1. Move the mouse so that the I-beam is in the left-hand margin alongside the line you wish to select, and the cursor will change to a selecting arrow (see below).

Okay, I think I am getting the hang of this now. I'll practise typing some more as I work through this book, page by page.

2. Click once and the selected **line** will be highlighted (see below).

Okay, I think I am getting the hang of this now. I'll practise typing some more as I work through this book, page by page.

3. To de-select the line, click anywhere in the document. (This method of de-selecting always applies to any selected text, picture or other item.)

Selecting a whole paragraph

Use the same procedure as when selecting a line, but **double**-click in the margin instead of single-clicking, and the entire paragraph will be selected and not just the line.

Selecting the entire document

There are two popular options for selecting all the text throughout an entire document – the Menu Bar method, and the keyboard shortcut method, which is faster.

> **Menu Bar method:**
>
> 1. On the **Menu Bar**, click on **Edit,** then on **Select All**, and everything in the entire document will be selected in the same highlighted manner.
> 2. Click anywhere in the document to de-select the text.

While using the Menu Bar method, on the **Edit** drop-down menu, to the right of the words **Select All**, notice the **Ctrl+A**. When you see a little note like this (or an icon) on a menu, it indicates a keyboard or Toolbar shortcut for that particular menu item. We'll use that Ctrl + A keyboard shortcut method now to select the entire document.

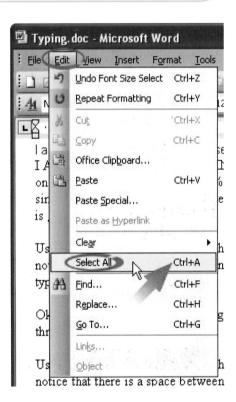

> **Keyboard shortcut method:**
>
> 1. On your keyboard, press `Ctrl` + `A` (**A** for All) and the entire document will be selected.
> 2. Click anywhere in the document to de-select it.

TIP: SELECTING AN ENTIRE DOCUMENT CAN BE VERY USEFUL

When you **Select All** by either of these two methods, the entire document is selected, no matter its length. This can be very useful, for example, if after typing a long document you decide to change the font size, colour or style throughout the whole document.

MOVING TO DIFFERENT PLACES IN A DOCUMENT

There are several ways to move around a document, depending on what you want to do.

Using the Scrollbars

If the page content is too long or too wide for the document window, you can use the Scrollbars to move up, down or across a page in order to bring the content into view. In Word you can use Scrollbars in many ways to move down or across the pages.

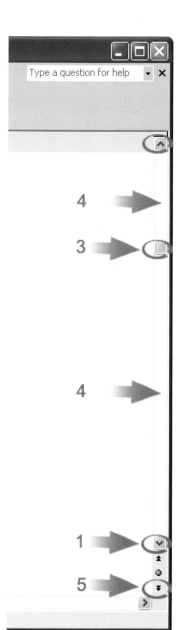

To scroll down:

1. Click repeatedly on the little ⌄ **Down** arrow (1) button at the bottom of the vertical Scrollbar, and the page will scroll down a little with each click; or

2. Keep the arrow depressed to continuously move the page down until you get to where you want to be; or

3. Click on the **solid shaded slider** (3), keep the mouse button depressed, and move the mouse towards you to **drag the** ▤ **slider downwards** and move on to the next pages of the document that are out of view; or

4. Click anywhere in the trough below the slider (4) to move the next page into view; or

5. Click on the **Next Page** double-arrow button (5) at the bottom of the Scrollbar to scroll one full page at a time.

To scroll up:

1. Follow points 1 to 5 above, but do everything in the opposite direction (⌃ **Up** arrow button, or the trough **above** the slider, and so on) and the page will scroll up instead of down. (The double-arrow **Next Page** and **Previous Page** buttons at the bottom of the vertical Scrollbar also enable you to scroll down or up a full page at a time.)

To scroll right or left:

1. Use the Scrollbar across the bottom of the Word window, and follow a similar procedure to move horizontally across a page to see more of the page.

Using the keyboard Page Up and Page Down buttons

1. Press the `PgU` **Page Up** or `PgD` **Page Down** key on the keyboard to move up or down, about half a page at a time.

Keyboard shortcuts to specific positions in the document

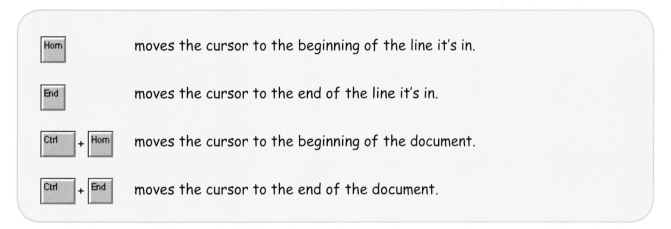

`Hom` moves the cursor to the beginning of the line it's in.

`End` moves the cursor to the end of the line it's in.

`Ctrl` + `Hom` moves the cursor to the beginning of the document.

`Ctrl` + `End` moves the cursor to the end of the document.

COPYING AND MOVING TEXT

Sometimes it's necessary to copy or move text around within a document, for example:
- to take a section of content in the document and repeat it elsewhere; or
- to cut a section of a document from where it is and 'paste' it somewhere else in the document, or even into a different document altogether.

The procedures for cutting, copying and pasting text are given on the next two pages.

Making a copy of the selected text

1. Using the text you've already typed, **double**-click in the left-hand margin next to the paragraph starting: `Using a computer...` in order to select that paragraph (see illustration below).

2. **Right**-click on the selected paragraph to open a little drop-down menu of options. (Alternatively, you could use the Menu Bar to click on **Edit** and open up the same little menu shown below.)

3. In that little menu, click on **Copy**, and the menu will close as if nothing has happened. However, an invisible copy of that paragraph has now been placed in the computer's memory section called the **Clipboard**, ready to be pasted anywhere.

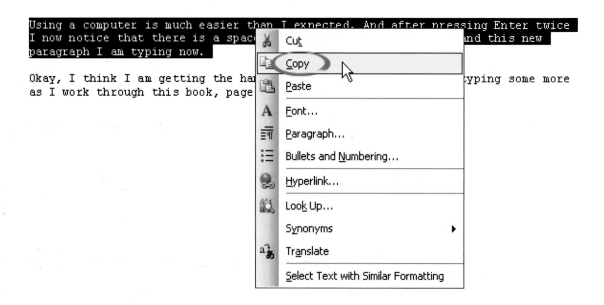

Pasting the copied text

Let's assume you want to paste the copied text right at the end of the document.

1. Press [Ctrl] + [End] to move the cursor to the end of the document.
2. Press [Enter] to create the starting point of a new paragraph.
3. On the **Menu Bar** click on **Edit**, then on **Paste**, and the text that has been copied to the Clipboard will appear at the end of the document.

TIP: SHORTCUTS FOR CUTTING, COPYING AND PASTING

Note the icons shown on the list of menu options. These indicate that there are also Toolbar shortcuts available. You can use those Toolbar buttons or one of the keyboard shortcuts to cut, copy or paste various items such as text, images, tables and other objects in a document. You can also copy an item from one document and paste it into another document. (You first need to select/highlight an item before you can copy it to the Clipboard.)

Keyboard shortcut	Toolbar shortcut	Effect
Ctrl + X	✂	**Cuts** (removes) the selected item from the document and puts it into the Clipboard Memory, ready for pasting elsewhere.
Ctrl + C	📋	**Copies** the selected item to the Clipboard memory, leaving the original where it is.
Ctrl + V	📋	**Pastes** the item in the Clipboard memory into the document, at the place where the cursor is. (It can be pasted over and over again if necessary.)

Toolbar Buttons, from left to right: Cut, Copy, Paste

NOTE: WORD PASTES ONLY THE LAST CLIPBOARD ITEM

When you copy or cut to the Clipboard, the previous item on the Clipboard will be replaced with the latest item copied or cut. So when you next paste, only the most recently copied/cut item will be pasted into the document.

ALIGNING TEXT

You can use keyboard shortcuts to align text in four basic ways. The default setting is usually to have text left-aligned – that is, with all lines of text flush against the left-hand margin. Here are the four options.

Left aligned	Ctrl + L **OR** [icon]	The left edge of the text is aligned flush against the left-hand margin. The right edge is not aligned. This is the normal default setting for documents and is used in many books.
Centre aligned	Ctrl + E **OR** [icon]	The text is centred on the page with no alignment on the left or the right. This is often used for document headings, menus, greeting cards, and so on.
Right aligned	Ctrl + R **OR** [icon]	The right edge of the text is flush against the right-hand margin. The left edge is not aligned. This is used, for example, for the address at the top of a typed letter.
Left and right justified	Ctrl + J **OR** [icon]	Both the left and right edges of the text are neatly aligned against their margins. This sometimes results in wider gaps between some words as Word stretches the text to fill a line. (This option is not available in WordPad.)

Once you've aligned some text, you can use these shortcuts to change any particular paragraph to have its own alignment that is different from the rest of the document. You can do this either before typing the paragraph or by selecting it after it's been typed.

Changing alignment before typing a new paragraph:

1. Use the appropriate shortcut as shown above and start typing.
2. To change again for the next paragraph, use a different shortcut and continue typing.

Changing alignment of an existing paragraph:

1. Click anywhere in the paragraph.
2. Use the appropriate keyboard shortcut as shown above and the paragraph's text will be aligned accordingly.

NOTE: PARAGRAPH FORMATTING VIA THE MENU BAR

You can also change paragraph alignment via the Menu Bar:

Click on **Format**, then **Paragraph**.

The **Paragraph** dialog box that opens gives you access

to other paragraph formatting as well.

ALIGNMENT EXERCISE:

1. Using the text you've already typed, click anywhere in one of the paragraphs.
2. Press `Ctrl` + `E` to centre the whole paragraph.
3. Click on the paragraph again.
4. Press `Ctrl` + `R` to right-align the paragraph.
5. Press `Ctrl` + `A` to select the entire document.
6. On the Menu Bar click on **Format**, then **Paragraph,** and select some of the options listed.
7. Click on **OK** and see the changes in your document.

USING BULLETS OR NUMBERS TO CREATE ITEMISED LISTS

Using **bullets** or **numbers** is a useful way to list points or numbered paragraphs in a neatly indented layout.

o This is a neat list of bullet points.
 o A new bullet appears when a new paragraph is created with the Enter key.
 o Word offers a range of different bullet and number styles.
	• This is the most frequently used style of bullet.
	 • It is also possible to have a sub-bullet like this:
	   – To do this, one needs to use the Format menu.
	   – This is found on the Menu Bar.
		1. Word offers the option to change the format of numbering too.
		 2. Sub-paragraph numbers are also possible:
		   i. This is done via the Format menu too.
		   ii. Explore this later.

To start a list of bulleted paragraphs:

> 1. On the **Formatting Toolbar**, click on the ⦙☰ **Bullets** icon.

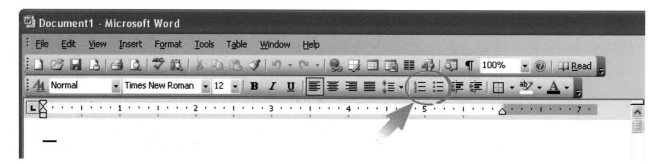

Numbering and Bullets buttons on the Formatting Toolbar

> 2. **Type this:** Bullets can be very useful.
> 3. **Press** [Enter] to create a new bullet point.
> 4. **Type this:** A new bullet requires a new paragraph.
> 5. **Press** [Enter] to create a new bullet point.
> 6. **Type this:** If I press Enter again without typing anything, no bullet will appear in the new paragraph.
> 7. **Press** [Enter] **twice** to start a new paragraph with no bullet.

USING AUTOMATIC PAGE NUMBERING

It can be very frustrating when a long printed document falls on the floor or out of the printer tray and the pages get all mixed up and have to be resorted – and there are no page numbers to help you. So make a habit of always inserting page numbers in any document that is longer than one page. Once you've done this, Word automatically numbers every page for you, in the position and text format you've selected.

1. On the **Menu Bar**, click on **Insert**, then **Page Numbers...** to open the **Page Numbers** dialog box.
2. In the dialog box, click on the little drop-down arrows to select the desired **Position:** and **Alignment:** of the page numbers.
3. To have **no** page number on the first page, click on the checkbox **Show number on first page** to remove the tick. (If you later decide that you *do* want a number on the first page you can click in the checkbox again to select that option.)

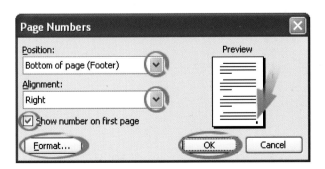

Note that the little Preview screen indicates where the page number will appear.

4. Click on **Format...** (bottom left of the Page Numbers dialog box in the previous screenshot) to select other page numbering options.

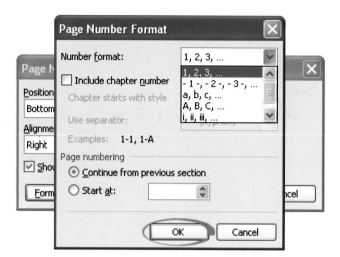

5. When done, click on **OK** to close the **Page Number Format** dialog box and then on **OK** to close the **Page Numbers** dialog box; all pages in this particular document will now be numbered automatically.

There are many more interesting and useful things that can be achieved with Microsoft Word; too many to be included in this introductory Book. However, if you need to enhance your Microsoft Word skills further you are welcome to visit the Discussion Forum at our Web site (see page 91) where you can ask questions for others to answer.

In the three chapters that follow you'll learn how to explore the Internet and how to send and receive electronic mail (e-mail).

3 The Internet

WHAT IS THE INTERNET?

In simple terms, the Internet is a worldwide network of millions of computers that can access one another via other high-capacity computers called *servers*, depicted as the three grey boxes in the illustration below. This communication is achieved via the existing worldwide network of telephone lines, cable and satellites – the same network that we use to make phone calls and send faxes.

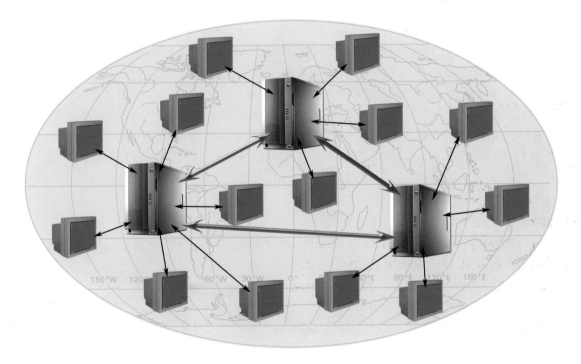

The Internet – a worldwide network of linked computers

To connect to this network, a home user or business signs up with an Internet Service Provider (ISP). This normally involves paying a monthly subscription. The ISP's servers are linked to other servers around the world, as depicted by the red data communication lines in the illustration above. These servers also store thousands of Web pages and other files that can be accessed by the other servers around the world. So in this way home and business users are able to view those millions of files by connecting to the Internet via their local ISP.

To be linked into the Internet from your own computer you need to sign up with one of the numerous service providers in your country. If you're not already connected to the Internet, browse the yellow pages or ask friends to recommend a reliable ISP.

POPULAR USES OF THE INTERNET

The two most popular uses of the Internet by the general public are:
- accessing a wealth of information and entertainment via *Web sites*;
- communicating with others by *e-mail* and other online communication systems.

We'll cover both of these in the next two chapters.

NOTE: IF YOU ALREADY HAVE INTERNET ACCESS

If you're using a computer that's already been set up with an Internet connection you can jump straight to the next chapter. Otherwise read through the guidelines below in order to get your computer set up for Internet access.

THREE KEY REQUIREMENTS FOR INTERNET ACCESS AND E-MAIL

Windows XP provides the programs necessary to make use of the Internet – Internet Explorer, a *browser* for browsing around the World Wide Web, and Outlook Express, which is used for sending and receiving e-mail. There are also three other essential requirements for getting connected to the Internet:

1. **A modem** – a connection device that will enable your computer to send and receive data via a telephone or cable line. Most new computers above entry level have an internal modem installed inside the tower; if not you'll need to have one installed or buy an external modem (see example on the right).

2. **An Internet Service Provider (ISP)** – through whose servers you'll be able to access the Internet, and who will provide you with your own e-mail address, user name and a password for logging in.

3. **Internet connection settings** – set up on your computer so that it can connect to your ISP via the modem or router (see note at the top of the next page).

Back view of computer and a modem (right) showing how they connect with telephone cables

> **NOTE: HIGH-SPEED CONNECTION REQUIRES A ROUTER**
>
> If you're opting for a high-speed connection, your ISP will most likely supply the router (at a price) with instructions on how to connect it to your computer and your telephone jack or cable. Usually this requires the telephone or cable company to make some physical changes to your phone line and wall connection or cable box.

This might all sound a little daunting at first but it's actually quite easy because once you have an Internet Service Provider they'll be able to help you configure your Internet connection and e-mail settings.

CHOOSING AN INTERNET PACKAGE THAT SUITS YOUR NEEDS

ISP's generally offer a range of options at different prices. So first decide what your needs are before making the call to sign up with an ISP.
- How many hours per month do you want to be connected?
- Do you want to connect only for brief periods just to send and collect your e-mails?
- Do you want to be connected all the time at one flat monthly fee?
- Will you be using e-mail to send large files to others via a high-speed connection such as ADSL (Asymmetric Digital Subscriber Line)?

High-speed (or *broadband*) ADSL works by splitting your existing telephone line's signal into two, one for voice and the other for data. The most popular high-speed services at the moment are running approximately nine times faster than a telephone dial-up connection with a modem. Therefore ADSL is useful for speedily sending or receiving large graphic files via the Internet and for faster access to and viewing of Web sites on the Internet.

Once you know your needs you'll know whether a dial-up modem to a standard telephone line or a high-speed router through an ADSL line will be the better option.

CHOOSING AN INTERNET SERVICE PROVIDER

We suggest that you don't sign up with just any ISP simply because they're inexpensive. Ask friends or work colleagues which ISP they use and ask if they're happy with the services and the pricing. Do they have a 24-hour Help line you can call if you need help? Are their connection lines always accessible or is there often a 'busy' signal when one tries to connect? Get recommendations and choose an ISP that has a reputable standing. Subscriptions vary around the world but it's usually not necessary to take out a subscription for a long period such as six months or a year. The norm is a monthly subscription that can be cancelled at any time.

SETTING UP YOUR INTERNET CONNECTION AND E-MAIL SETTINGS

The usual quick and easy way to set up the connection and your e-mail account settings on your computer is to call your Internet Service Provider (ISP) and ask them to talk you through the setting-up process over the phone. Alternatively, follow the instructions that came with your ISP's welcoming pack or CD, if you were given one.

CREATING A DIAL-UP SHORTCUT ON YOUR DESKTOP

It's useful to create a shortcut icon on your Desktop so that you can double-click on it to connect your computer to the Internet through your Internet Service Provider.

1. Click on **start** and point to **Connect To**.
2. In the sub-menu that opens, **right**-click on the **Internet connection** displayed (ours shows **Beltel Dialup**) to open up the next sub-menu.
3. Click on **Create Shortcut**.

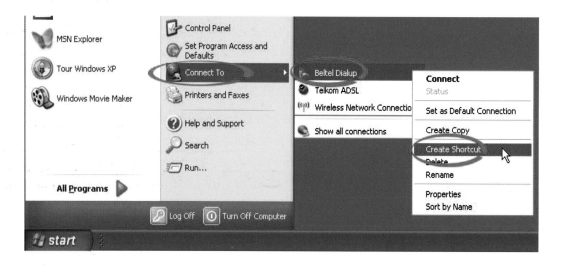

4. In the **Shortcut** dialog box that opens, click on **Yes** and Windows will place the shortcut on your Desktop.

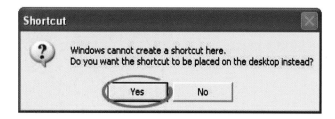

Typical dialup shortcut

Typical broadband shortcut

CONNECTING TO THE INTERNET

Once your modem or router has been set up and you have signed up with an ISP for an Internet subscription, you're ready to connect to the Internet. If you've set your system up to be connected 24 hours a day, then when you start up your computer it will automatically connect to the Internet. Otherwise follow the procedure given below.

1. Click on each open program's
    Close button to close all programs and get back to the Desktop.
2. On the Desktop find your **Internet connection shortcut** and **double**-click on the icon to open the **Connect** dialog box.

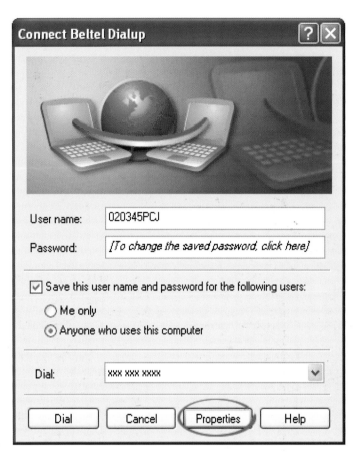

Protecting your system against viruses

> ! **PROTECT YOUR COMPUTER**
> Before you connect to the Internet for the first time it's wise to make sure you have the basic Windows XP Internet protection setting enabled. It's called a *Firewall* and it helps to limit or prevent access to your computer by viruses and spyware that can be annoying at best, or even cause malfunctions of your software.

3. Click on **Properties** (see previous screenshot) to open the **Properties** dialog box.

4. Click on the **Advanced** tab.

5. Click on **Settings...** to open the **Windows Firewall** dialog box.

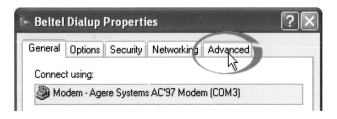

6. In the **Windows Firewall** dialog box, if the **On (recommended)** radio button is not selected (no green dot in the white circle), click on it to select it.

7. Click on **OK** to close the **Windows Firewall** dialog box, then click on **OK** in the Properties dialog box to get back to the **Connect** dialog box.

8. Back in the **Connect** dialog box, click on **Dial** (for Dial-up connection) or on **Connect** if you have a broadband connection that is not 'enabled' to auto-connect when you turn your computer on, and Windows will start connecting you to the Internet.

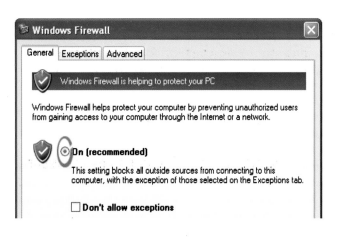

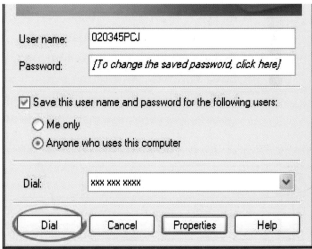

It will take several seconds before you're connected to your ISP. Once you're connected you'll see an icon on the right of your Taskbar at the bottom of the screen showing two little computer monitors with blue screens (which may be flashing intermittently as data is moving between your computer and your ISP's server). This flashing icon indicates that you're connected to your ISP and therefore to the Internet.

'Connected' icon
on Taskbar

DISCONNECTING FROM THE INTERNET

1. On the Taskbar, **right**-click on the little icon showing the two computer monitors.
2. In the menu that opens (see screenshot on the right), click on **Disconnect**.
3. Make sure the little computers icon has disappeared; this confirms that you are now 'offline'.

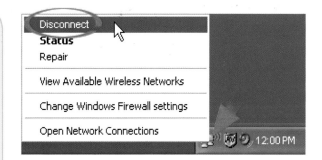

TIP: GETTING HELP FROM YOUR ISP

If you have any problems connecting to the Internet call your Internet Service Provider's **Help** line and ask them to check the relevant settings for you over the telephone. This is normal practice so there's no need to feel inadequate or ignorant.

Once you know you have an Internet connection that's working, you're ready to start having fun.

 IF YOU'RE PAYING PER MINUTE, REMEMBER TO DISCONNECT
If you're on dial-up and are paying per minute for being connected to the telephone line, remember to disconnect from the Internet once you've finished with your Internet activities.

In the next chapter you'll be 'surfing the Net' almost immediately and finding some interesting stuff on the World Wide Web. Let's go!

4 Surfing the Internet

In this chapter you'll be surfing the Internet in no time and accessing all sorts of weird and wonderful Web sites. It is nothing short of mind-boggling to see how one can sit in the comfort of one's own home and be able to enjoy such a rich mix of information, visual and sound experiences, as well as news and entertainment via the World Wide Web.

WHAT IS THE WORLD WIDE WEB?

The World Wide Web is a part of the Internet where one can access millions of files located on nearly as many computers linked worldwide through the Internet – text, photographs and other images, as well as sound and video files.

Accessing this massive worldwide library of information is done by means of a computer software program called a *browser,* which enables you to browse the Web to see what interests you. This is what people mean when they say they're *surfing the Net.* This is much the same as going to a library and browsing through the catalogues and shelves to find books of interest to you.

Anyone can make their own information available for browsing by others too; it's not simply a commercial or academic network. People have their family history, photo albums and lots of personal information they want to share with the world, not to mention some of the 'other' stuff that many would prefer not to be exposed to, if you know what we mean. ☺

The Web *browser* that is most widely used worldwide is, without doubt, Microsoft's *Internet Explorer,* which comes bundled with Windows XP.

CONNECTING TO THE INTERNET

Before you can access the World Wide Web you'll need to connect to the Internet first, using the procedure explained in the previous chapter (page 57):

1. Close all open program windows so that you can see the Desktop.
2. **Double**-click on the shortcut icon for your Internet connection.
3. In the **Connect** dialog box that opens, click on **Dial** (for Dial-up connection) or on **Connect** if you have a broadband connection that is not 'enabled' to auto-connect when you turn your computer on.
4. Wait for the connection to be made (the little computer screens icon will appear on the right-hand section of your Taskbar at the bottom of your screen).

Shortcut icon
on the Desktop

OPENING INTERNET EXPLORER

1. If you don't see the shortcut icon for Internet Explorer on your desktop (that you can double-click on to open your browser), click on **start** then **All Programs** then **Internet Explorer** to open your browser which will immediately display its default 'home' Web page, usually the Microsoft Web site if this is the first time Internet Explorer has been opened. (We suggest you follow the procedure already explained to create a Desktop shortcut to Internet Explorer for future use.)

2. Note the Web site address shown in the **Address** window, just above the Web page being displayed.

Example of a Web page

NOTE: SOMETIMES THE PROGRAM INVITES A DIAL-UP

Internet Explorer is sometimes set up so that if you load it before connecting to the Internet a dialog box opens inviting you to connect. (Outlook Express operates similarly if it's been set up that way.) The independent dial-up/connect desktop shortcut we've suggested, however, allows you to connect to the Internet *without* first having to load your Web browser or your e-mail program. We prefer that independent dial-up shortcut method because it allows you to use other Internet programs such as Instant Messaging and Internet telephony without having to load Internet Explorer or Outlook Express in order to connect to the Internet.

THREE MAIN APPROACHES TO THE WEB

People visit a public library for several reasons:
- to find a specific book they want to read;
- to look for information on a particular subject; or
- to browse the shelves to see if there's anything that interests them enough to want to read more about it.

The World Wide Web is used in a similar way, except that the browsing involves digital information stored on computers – and you can do it from the comfort of your own home.

The first thing we'll do is show you how to get to a specific Web site where you already know the World Wide Web (www) address. For this task we'll take you to the companion Web site of the Really, Really, Really Easy Computer Books. You can then follow the same procedures to visit any other Web sites you might know about.

GOING TO A SPECIFIC WEB SITE

NOTE: WEB SITE ADDRESS FORMATS

Every Web site has a unique address on the Internet – termed a URL (Uniform Resource Locator) – that specifies the exact computer location of that Web page on the World Wide Web. The full format of a Web site or Web page address is usually (though not always) something like **http://www.reallyeasycomputerbooks.com**. The **http://** describes the type of access method being used. The next part, **www.reallyeasycomputerbooks. com**, is a pointer to the computer or resource that hosts the Web site. It is not *always* necessary to type the **http://** in front of the **www**.

1. In Internet Explorer, click anywhere inside the white **Address** window below the Menu Bar to select the address currently shown, so that you can replace it with this computer book's Web site address.
2. Type the following into that window, with no full stop at the end:
    `www.reallyeasycomputerbooks.com`
3. **Check the spellings very carefully – note** the full stops after **www** and before **com**, and note that there are **no** spaces between any letters. (This is standard practice for Web site addresses.)
4. When you're happy that you have the address spelt exactly as it should be, press
    Enter and Internet Explorer will take you to that address within seconds. (The image on your screen may look slightly different from the one shown.)

5. Look at the left of the grey strip at the bottom of the browser window (the **Status Bar**) to see when the Web page has fully loaded; it will usually display the word **Done**.

NAVIGATING WEB PAGES

You can move from page to page by clicking on what are called *hyperlinks* (or simply *links*, for short). Some links take you to a heading somewhere else on the page, others may take you to another page at the same site, while yet others may take you to a different Web site altogether. The following are typical ways in which links may appear on a Web page:

- underlined text;
- text that is not underlined but might be in bold or a different font colour;
- images such as logos, photos and so on;
- items in a menu list;
- tabs on one of the edges of the Web page.

When you move the mouse pointer over any link, no matter which of the above-mentioned formats it takes, the pointer will change its shape into a hand.

Let's move from our site's home page to the first main page of the site.

1. Move the mouse pointer over the image on our home page and notice how the pointer changes shape, indicating that the image is a link to another page.

2. Click on the words **Enter Site** (or on the image) and wait for the linked page to load.

3. In the screenshot below, notice the three types of links used: underlined headings, images, and tabs at the top of the page.

4. Place the pointer over each link in turn to see it change shape to a  hand.

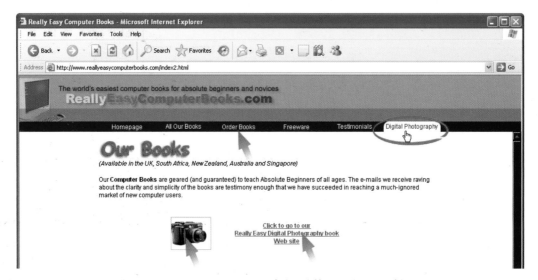

The red arrows show some of the different kinds of links

5. To reveal more of the lower part of the page use the **Scrollbar** on the right.

Once you've visited some Web pages you can move back and forth between them by clicking on the **Back** and **Forward** buttons on the browser's Toolbar.

Back button   Forward button

6. On the Toolbar click on the **Back** button to go to the previous page.

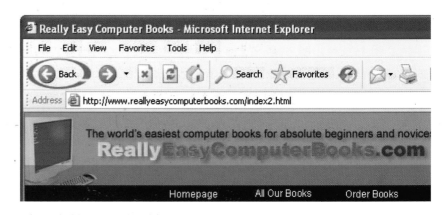

BOOKMARKING A SITE FOR FUTURE VISITS

If you find a useful Web site – or a specific page at that site – that you know you'll want to visit again, you can get Internet Explorer to remember the address for you and store it in a menu called **Favorites**. Let's practice by adding our Really Easy Computer Books to your **Favorites:**

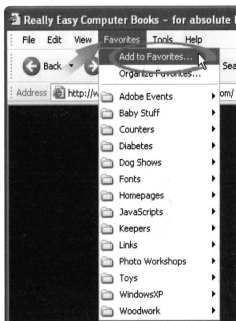

1. On the browser's Menu Bar (see right), click on **Favorites**, then on **Add To Favorites...** and the **Add Favorite** dialog box will open (screenshot below).
2. Click on **OK** and the Web page address will be added to your list of **Favorites**.

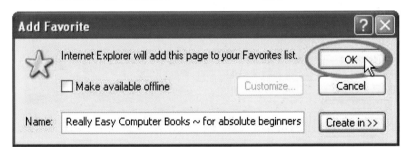

TIP: YOU CAN FILE YOUR FAVORITES IN FOLDERS

To find your **Favorites** quickly in the future, you can save them to topic-related folders that you can create yourself. To do this, before clicking on **OK** in Step 2 above, click on the **Create in >>** button below it to extend the dialog box; then click on **New Folder...**, type the name you want to give the folder and click on **OK** to get back to the **Add Favorite** dialog box. Click on **OK** again to save your new **Favorite** page to that folder. You can add other related **Favorites** to that same folder in future.

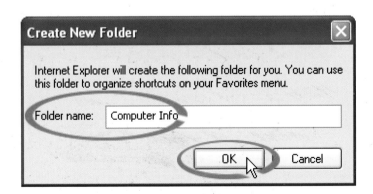

---

3. On the Toolbar (see below) click on the **Home** icon to go back to the browser's home page for the next topic.

Home button takes you to your browser's home page

NOTE: ABOUT HOME PAGES

The main page of any Web site is called its **Home Page**. Just to confuse us all, the default page to which your browser goes when it is first opened is also called a Home Page.

GOING STRAIGHT TO ONE OF YOUR FAVOURITE WEB PAGES

1. On the Menu Bar click on **Favorites**, then on the folder you want (if you have created folders) – in our case **Computer Info**.

2. Click on the saved Web page address you require – **Really Easy Computer Books** – and you'll be taken back to our Web page.

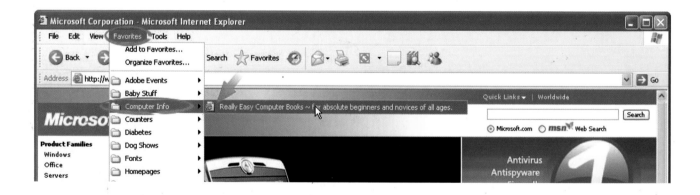

SEARCHING THE WEB FOR INFORMATION

You would think that finding what you're looking for in a worldwide network of millions of computer files would be an extremely difficult task. Well, thanks to creative software programmers, we have *search engines* that make this task pretty easy, even for a beginner – in fact, possibly even easier than finding something in a large public library, and certainly much, much faster.

We'll use one of the world's most popular search engines; it's called Google.

1. Click anywhere in the **Address** window of Internet Explorer to select the existing address that's there, so that you can type over it to replace it.

2. Type this: `http://www.google.com`

3. Press [Enter] and you'll be taken straight to the Google Web site.

4. While you're there, on the Menu Bar, click on **Favorites** to check whether Google is listed; if it's not, add it to your **Favorites** (see page 65).

5. In the Google text window, type any topic that interests you in any format, in upper or lower case (examples: `table mountain; bagpipes; ufo; planting trees; Princess Diana; bird flu; solar eclipse; fixing motorcycles; buying a computer`).

6. Press [Enter] or click on the [Google Search] button, and a page listing Web sites that match your search criteria will open in your browser (see below).

   Don't be shocked at how many pages and Web sites there are!

7. Read through the list of sites on the left of the page, and click on any one that catches your interest.

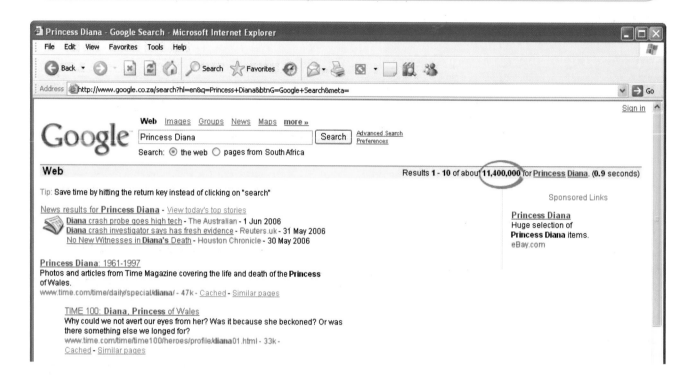

8. If there's nothing in view that seems to match what you're specifically looking for, use the Scrollbar on the right to scroll down to the bottom of the page.

9. At the bottom of the page, click on **Next** to move to the next page (or click on the **Next** arrow or on the next **page number** in the sequence of pages shown).

Narrowing down a search

There are several ways to fine-tune a search so that the Web sites displayed are more closely related to the specific topic you're looking for. Like most search engines, Google offers an **Advanced Search** option that can be clicked on.

TIP: READ THE ADVANCED SEARCH TIPS

For additional tips on advanced searches with Google on the Advanced Search page, click on the **Advanced Search Tips** link.

Searching a new topic

1. To search for something different, click on the browser's ⬅ Back ▾ button until you're back at a Google search window, and start a new search.
2. Click on the other Google search links at the top of the browser window too, and explore what's available – e.g. searches for images only.

NOTE: THERE ARE OTHER SEARCH ENGINES TOO

Google is not the only search facility available. There are some that use a selection of other search engines to get a wider search sweep. To find some alternative search engines and Web directories do a Google search for **Search Engines**.

PERSONAL INTERNET SECURITY

Being connected to millions of computer users around the world makes you vulnerable to invasions of your privacy and security through invasive programs called *spyware*. It also puts your computer at risk of being hijacked by some malicious program that could interfere with some key system files and cause your system to 'crash' and not function properly. These programs are called *viruses*. Here are some important tips to help you protect your personal privacy and security as well as your computer system. We urge you to take these suggestions seriously.

- Protect your system *without delay* by making sure your Windows Firewall is enabled (see page 58), and by having effective anti-virus and anti-spyware programs installed immediately. (Our Web site has some suggestions in this regard.) Don't download and install <u>any</u> programs, free offers, screensavers or novelties until this has been done.

- Visit our Web site at **http://www.reallyeasycomputerboks.com** for useful tips and links to help you protect your privacy and security.

REMEMBER TO DISCONNECT

If you're on a dial-up connection, and particularly if you're paying per minute while you're connected to the Internet, remember to disconnect when you're finished surfing the Net (see page 59).

In Book 2 we'll show you some more useful tips and step-by-step procedures including, for example, how to download useful free programs from the Internet; how to save ink when printing a Web page, and more.

In the next chapter you'll learn how to use your Internet connection to exchange letters and files with friends, family or work colleagues anywhere in the world, using e-mail.

5 E-mail

WHAT IS E-MAIL?

E-mail is short for electronic mail. It is the digital way of sending correspondence between two or more people anywhere in the world using computers that are linked to the Internet.

E-mail is very fast indeed – a letter sent from London can be read by the recipient on the other side of the planet within seconds of its having been sent. And if it's addressed to several recipients, they'll all receive it virtually simultaneously, no matter where in the world they're located, as long as they have a computer that's connected to the Internet.

This makes e-mail a very exciting medium for communicating with family, friends and business associates worldwide. With e-mail you can send normal text as well as formatted items such as Word documents, full-colour photographs, company brochures, slide presentations, and even sound and video files.

The program we'll use for e-mail is one that comes as part of the Windows XP operating system; it's called **Outlook Express**.

SETTING UP YOUR E-MAIL ACCOUNT

Besides an Internet connection – that connects your computer to your ISP's host computer (see Chapter 3) – to be able to send and receive e-mail you'll also need to be able to connect to your own personal electronic mail box on your ISP's **mail server**. To do this, an e-mail account needs to be set up in Outlook Express using the information provided to you by your Internet Service Provider. This is usually done over the phone with your ISP or from their welcome pack instructions. If you haven't yet done this, now is the time to call your ISP's technical support team and ask them to take you through the process. To do this you'll need to open Outlook Express.

> **TIP: WRITE YOUR LOG-IN DETAILS ON PAGE 92**
> It's a good idea to keep a note of all log-in details written down somewhere in case something should happen to your computer and you lose the data. Use the list on page 92 for this purpose.

OPENING OUTLOOK EXPRESS

1. Click on **start** then **All Programs**, then **Outlook Express** and your e-mail program (or 'e-mail client', as it's often called) will open on the Desktop.

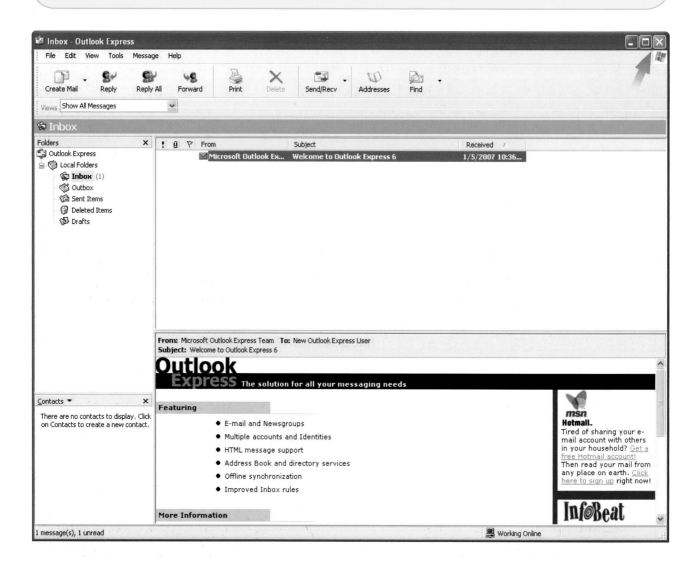

WRITING AN E-MAIL

Once your e-mail account has been set up, you're ready to write an e-mail. With Outlook Express open on your screen, follow these easy steps:

1. On the Outlook Express **Toolbar** click on **Create Mail**.

A **New Message** window will open with the cursor flashing in the **To:** window, ready for you to type the recipient's e-mail address.

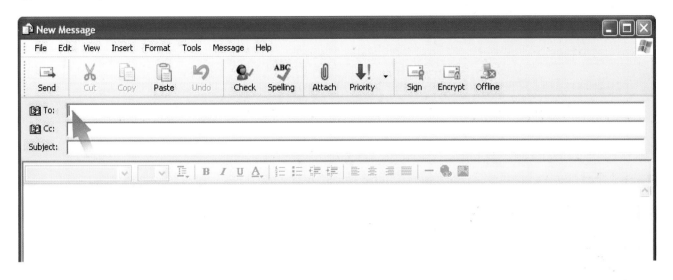

NOTE: IF YOU CAN'T SEE ALL THE TOOLBAR BUTTONS

If you can't see all the buttons on the Formatting Toolbar, click on the Maximize button in the top right-hand corner of Outlook Express to maximize the window to full-screen view.

---

2. In the **To:** window type the **e-mail address** of the person you're sending the e-mail to, being careful to type it accurately.

TIP: E-MAIL ADDRESSES

The standard format of an e-mail address is the recipient's e-mail name, followed by the @ symbol, which is then typically followed by the domain name of their service provider (unless they have an e-mail address reflecting their own or business's domain name). Be sure to leave **no** spaces between any of the address components. It needs to be 100% accurate or the e-mail won't reach the recipient and instead will 'bounce' back to you. Format examples: gavin@reallyeasybooks.com, joshua.smith@yahoo.uk.com

---

3. Press the ⎄ key repeatedly until the cursor is in the **Subject:** window, and type a meaningful subject for your e-mail.

4. Press the ⎄ key again to move the cursor to the main message window (the large white space), and start typing your letter as you would type a document.

5. Note the formatting buttons that become available on the Formatting Toolbar when you've clicked in the message window, and use any that you need.

6. When done, click on **Send**.

7. If you have any spelling errors the spell checker will pop up; follow the prompts to change the spelling, ignore or add the word to the Outlook Express dictionary.

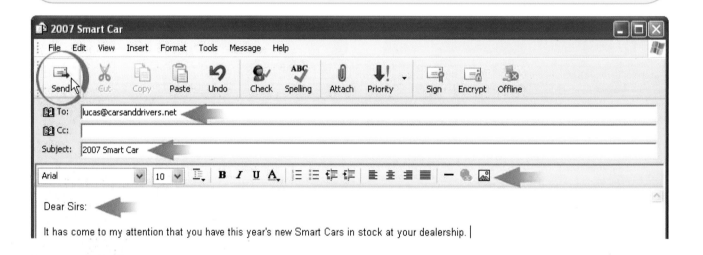

NOTE: CONNECT IN ORDER TO TRANSMIT

If you're connected to the Internet your letter will be transmitted as soon as you click on **Send**. If you're *not* connected, the letter will be sent to the **Outbox** waiting to be transmitted when you're next online (connected to the Internet).

NEED A TEST E-MAIL RECIPIENT?

If you want to test your e-mail system feel free to send an e-mail to this address:

test@reallyeasycomputerbooks.com

It is intentionally not a valid address so your e-mail will bounce back to you with a message that it could not be delivered. That's fine. At least you'll know it was sent and received by our mail server, which then sent you an automatic reply notifying you that you did not use a valid e-mail address.

ATTACHING A FILE TO YOUR E-MAIL

If you want to send someone a Word document you've typed, or a photo that's stored on your computer, or any other file for that matter, you simply send it as an attachment.

1. Create a new e-mail by filling in the **To:** and **Subject:** and **Message** windows.
2. On the Toolbar, click on the **Attach** button.

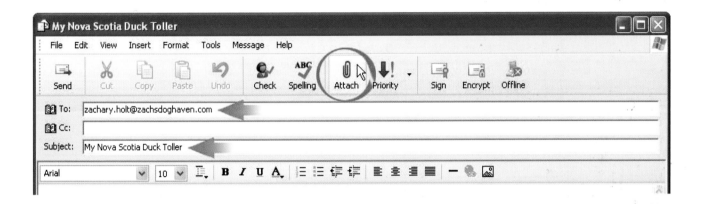

3. In the **Insert Attachment** dialog box that opens, click on the little ⌄ 'down' arrow in order to find the file you wish to attach. (Once selected, the file name also appears in the **File Name:** window next to the **Attach** button.)
4. **Double**-click on the file name (or click on it, then click on **Attach** or press [Enter]), and the file will be attached to your e-mail.

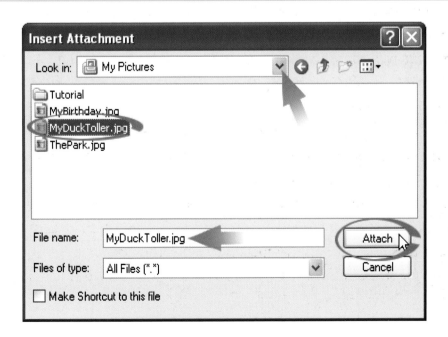

5. To make sure the file is attached, check that the file name appears in the **Attach:** window of the e-mail you're about to send.

6. Send your e-mail per the next procedure and it will transmit together with the attachment.

 DON'T SEND VERY LARGE ATTACHMENTS

Large attachments are not recommended for several reasons, including:

- They take a long time to transmit and also for the recipient to download to their computer from the mailbox on their ISP's mail server. This can be annoying for an unsuspecting recipient.
- Some ISPs place a limit on the file size of an e-mail that can be sent through their servers, so a very large file could cause problems.

Unless you have a special reason for sending a particular file that is large, try to avoid this as far as possible. The maximum size allowed by some ISPs is in the region of 1 to 2 Megabytes (MB). For suggestions on how to resize photographs for sending by e-mail, refer to our companion book, Really, Really, Really Easy Digital Photography, or visit this book's Web site and click on the 'Digital Photography' link.

SENDING AN E-MAIL

If you're not already connected to the Internet, and you have e-mails sitting in your Outbox waiting to be transmitted, here's what you do:

1. If Outlook Express is open on the Desktop (i.e. in view on your computer screen), click on the ▬ **Minimize** button to send Outlook Express down to the Taskbar so that you can see the Internet Connection shortcut on the Desktop.
2. Follow the procedure on page 60 to connect to the Internet.
3. Once you're connected, click on the ⬛ Inbox - Outlook Express **Outlook Express task button** on the Taskbar to restore the program to full-screen view.
4. In the **Folders** task pane on the left, click on **Outbox**.
5. On the Outlook Express Toolbar, click on the little ▾ **drop-down arrow** on the right of the **Send/Recv** button to open the drop-down menu.
6. Click on **Send All**, and the e-mail/s stored in your **Outbox** will be transmitted to the recipients via the Internet.

Your own copy of the sent e-mail will be moved automatically from the **Outbox** to the **Sent Items** mail box, where it will be stored for future reference until you delete it. To see your sent e-mails, click on the **Sent Items** folder on the left.

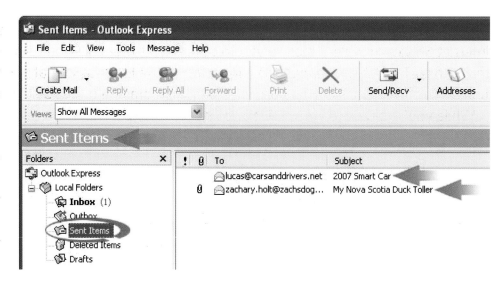

That's it! You've just successfully sent your first e-mail.

NOTE: YOU CAN SEND AND RECEIVE SIMULTANEOUSLY

Some people simply click on the **Send/Recv** button and collect all new mail at the same time as they're sending their outgoing mail. This may suit some users but we prefer to have more control over what happens. So we send mail when we decide to, and we collect our mail as a separate action – also when we decide to do so. Separating the **Send** and the **Receive** actions, as we have recommended, makes mail control easier. In addition, we recommend a free program that allows you to see what incoming mail is waiting for you on your ISP's mail server. You can delete any unwanted or suspicious mail before you download valid e-mails to your computer. More is said about this on this book's companion Internet Web site www.reallyeasycomputerbooks.com.

RECEIVING E-MAIL

When someone sends you paper mail the postal services deliver it to your post box, either the one at your home or a rented box at the post office. To read your mail you need to go and fetch it from the post box.

E-mail collection is similar, only it's electronic. You rent an e-mail box that is located on your Internet Service Provider's mail server. To read any new e-mails you need to fetch them from the mail server. To do this you must be connected to the Internet so that you can log in to your mail box and retrieve your mail. You use your e-mail program (e.g. Outlook Express) to do this.

While you're online (connected to the Internet) you can retrieve e-mail as follows:

1. On the Outlook Express Toolbar, click on the little ▾ **drop-down arrow** on the right of the **Send/Recv** button to open the drop-down menu (see previous screenshot).

2. Click on **Receive All**, and any e-mail/s on the mail server will be downloaded from the mail server to your Outlook Express **Inbox**.

DISCONNECTING FROM THE INTERNET

In some countries there's a per-minute cost for being connected to your ISP via a phone line, in which case users may wish to keep their online time as brief as possible. If this is your situation, remember to disconnect from the Internet once you've sent and received all your e-mails, unless you intend doing other things on the Internet, like visiting Web sites. Here's the disconnecting procedure again:

1. On the Taskbar, **right**-click on the little icon showing the two computer monitors.

2. In the menu that opens (see screenshot on the right), click on **Disconnect.**

3. Make sure the little icon has disappeared; this confirms that you are now 'offline'.

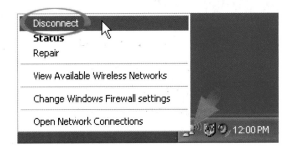

READING NEW MAIL

By default, all new incoming mail will be downloaded to your **Inbox**. You do not need to be connected to the Internet to read mail already downloaded from the server or to compose your mail. To read it:

1. Click on the **Inbox** to select it.

Note the following:
- The number of unopened e-mails is shown in brackets behind the word **Inbox**.
- The e-mails contained in the Inbox are listed in the window on the right. If your **Inbox** has lots of e-mails you can use the Scrollbar on the right to scroll through the list to see more of them.
- E-mails that have not been opened are shown in bold text.

---

2. To preview an e-mail **without** opening it, click on it in the list on the right, and it will be displayed in the preview pane below but without all the header details such as sender's e-mail address and so on.

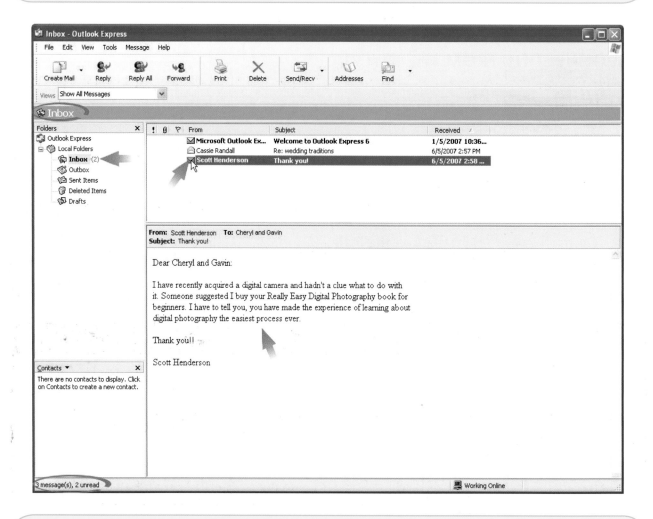

---

3. To open the e-mail fully, double-click on it in the **Inbox** list (or click on it and press Enter) and the e-mail will open in a separate window where you can read it, open any files attached to it, reply to it and so on.

4. Press the Esc key (or click on the ☒ **Close** button of the e-mail) to return to the **Inbox** contents list. (That e-mail will no longer be listed in bold.)

OPENING AND VIEWING ATTACHED FILES

Sometimes someone may send you an e-mail that has a file attached, such as a digital photograph, a Word document and so on. There are two ways to know that an e-mail includes an attachment – from the **Inbox** list or from the opened e-mail itself.

In the **Inbox** list of e-mails you might see a little paper clip to the left of the **From** column. This indicates that the e-mail has an attachment.

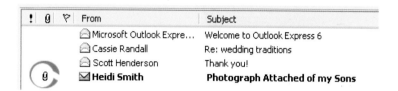

To view the attachment itself you need to open the e-mail and not just preview it in the Preview Pane.

1. **Double**-click on the e-mail that has the attachment in order to open the e-mail (or click on it and press Enter↵).
2. Note that the name of the attached file is shown in the **Attach:** window of the opened e-mail (see next screenshot).
3. **Double**-click on that file name to open the attachment (or click on it and press Enter↵).

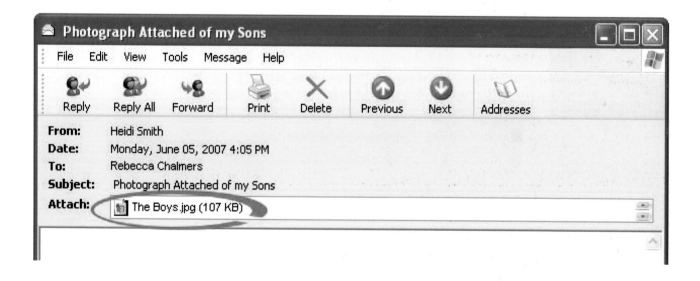

4. In the **Mail Attachment** dialog box that opens, if you're satisfied that the file is safe to open (has been checked by your up-to-date anti-virus scanner), click on **Open** and the file will open in the program appropriate to viewing that type of file.

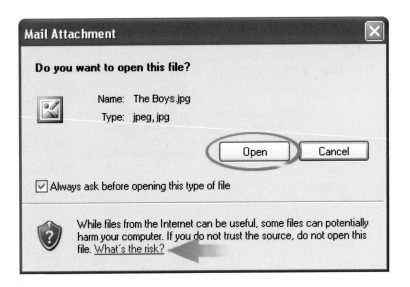

 BEWARE OF VIRUSES AND SECURITY RISKS

E-mail is another doorway to having viruses and spyware ending up on your computer.

*   If you receive any junk mail (called *spam mail* in Internet jargon) from people you don't know, just delete it.
*   Don't click on any 'Unsubscribe' links in spam e-mails you've received. Doing this simply confirms that your e-mail address is active.
*   If you receive an e-mail with a file attached to it, do <u>not</u> open the file unless your up-to-date anti-virus software scanned your mail as it came in.
*   Never respond to e-mails asking you to verify any personal details, such as your bank account or credit card details. There are many scams going on and the Internet is a wonderful place for fraudsters to hide behind anonymity.
*   Visit our Web site at http://www.reallyeasycomputerbooks.com for useful tips and links to help you protect your privacy and security.

DELETING E-MAILS

We suggest you make it a habit to delete e-mails you don't really need to keep. Otherwise your **Inbox** can become cluttered with old mails that you have to scroll through when you're looking for an important one later.

Deleting an open e-mail:

1. On the Toolbar at the top of the open e-mail, click on the **Delete** button.

Deleting e-mails in the list:

1. Click on the e-mail in order to select it.
2. Click on the Toolbar's **Delete** button or press the [Del] key on your keyboard.

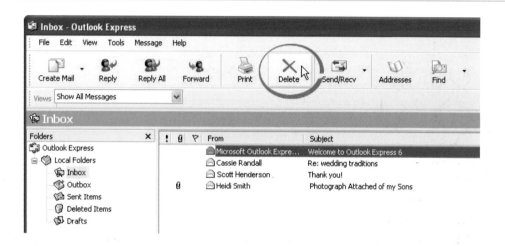

NOTE: IF YOU DELETE IN ERROR

If you deleted an e-mail in error, click on the **Deleted Items** mail box and move the e-mail back into the **Inbox** by clicking on it and, with the mouse button held down, dragging the pointer to the **Inbox**. When the **Inbox** is selected (blue), release the mouse button to drop the e-mail into the Inbox. **Important:** This must be done **before you close Outlook Express,** otherwise when you next load Outlook Express the **Deleted Items** mail box will be empty and the deleted items irretrievable.

Deleting several e-mails at once

1. To delete several e-mails simultaneously, hold down the [Ctrl] key; click on each e-mail in the list that you wish to delete, and each one will be selected (blue).
2. Press the [Del] key and they'll all be sent to the **Deleted Items** mail box.

REPLYING TO AN E-MAIL

1. Click on the e-mail in the **Inbox** list to select it, or double-click to open it.
2. On the Toolbar click on the **Reply** button and the Message window opens.

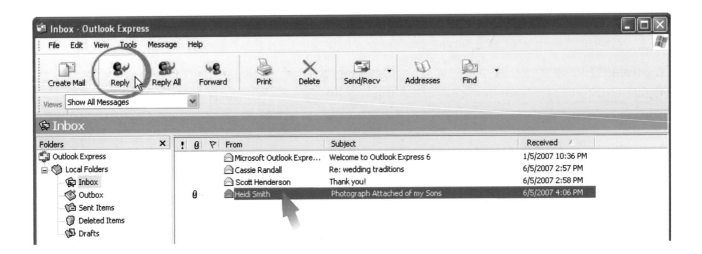

3. Type your reply.
4. On the Toolbar click on **Send**. (Make sure you're connected to the Internet.)

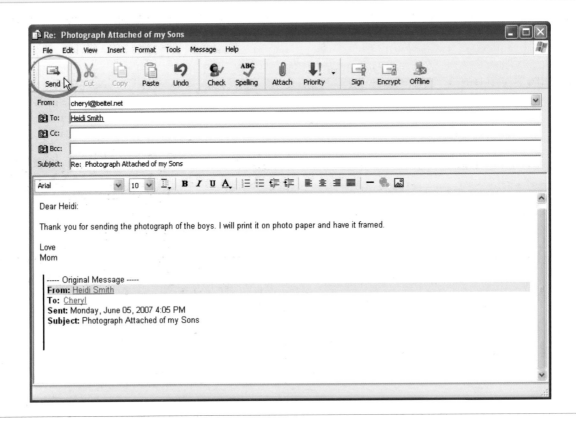

FORWARDING AN E-MAIL TO SOMEONE ELSE

To forward (or send) a received e-mail to someone other than the sender or any other recipients, you'll need to enter the new recipient's e-mail address in the **To:** window.

1. Open the e-mail or click on it in the **Inbox** list to select it.
2. On the Toolbar click on the **Forward** button.
3. In the **To:** window type the e-mail address of the new recipient.
4. In the main window type any comments you wish to add.
5. On the Toolbar click on **Send**. (Make sure you're connected to the Internet.)

SAVING AN ADDRESS IN THE ADDRESS BOOK

There are two ways you can save someone's e-mail address in your Outlook Express address book for future easy access – directly from an e-mail you've received, or by typing a new address into the book.

Saving directly from a received e-mail

1. In the **Inbox** click on the e-mail to select it, or **double**-click to open it.
2. On the Toolbar click on **Tools,** then on **Add Sender to Address Book** and Outlook Express will add that person's name and e-mail address to your address book. (The saving is done in the background so you won't see anything happening on the screen.)

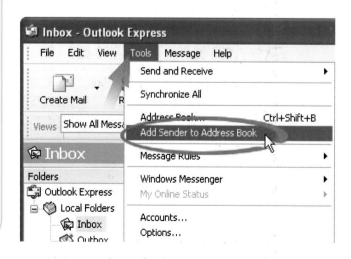

Entering a new address manually

1. On the Toolbar click on the **Addresses** button to open the **Address Book – Main Identity** dialog box. (If **Addresses** is not showing on the **Toolbar**, click on **Tools**, then on **Address Book**.)

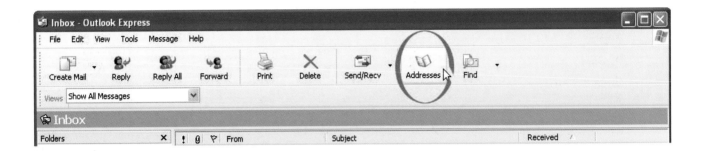

2. On the Toolbar of the **Address Book – Main Identity** dialog box that opens, click on **New**, then on **New Contact...**

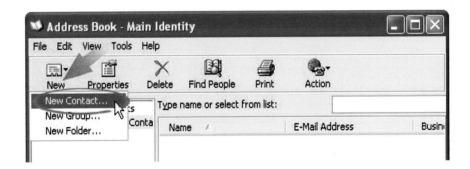

3. In the **Properties** dialog box that opens, click the **Name** tab if it's not already selected, type the person's first name, then press [Tab] each time you want to move to the next text window (last name, e-mail address, plus whatever additional information you want to assign this person).

4. Press **Tab** to move to the **E-Mail Addresses:** window and type the person's e-mail address. (As soon as you start typing in the **E-mail addresses:** window the **Add** button becomes active.)

5. Click on **Add**, then on **OK**, and the address will be added to the Address Book.

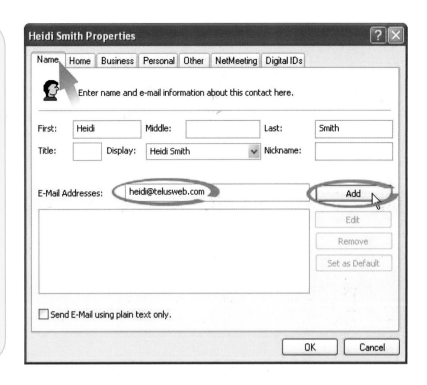

Note that once the address has been added, the **Edit**, **Remove** and **Set as Default** buttons become active in case you want to make changes to that entry at any time. Also, the e-mail address moves to the lower pane.

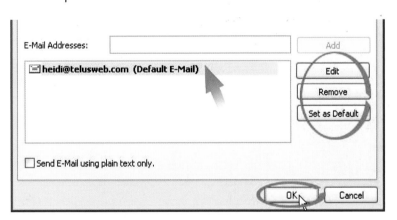

6. Click on **OK** or press **Enter** to close the Properties dialog box.

7. Repeat steps 2 to 6 should you wish to add another person's e-mail address.

8. When you've finished entering addresses, click on the ☒ **Close** button on the **Address Book – Main Identity** dialog box to close it.

USING THE ADDRESS BOOK WHEN CREATING A NEW E-MAIL

1. On the Toolbar, click on **Create Mail** to open the **New Mail** dialog box.
2. Start to type the recipient's name as it was entered into the address book and note how Outlook Express automatically completes the person's name for you. (It includes the e-mail address hidden in the background.)

MAKE SURE IT'S THE CORRECT RECIPIENT
If you have more than one person with that first name, Outlook Express may not offer the one you're looking for; so be sure you select the correct recipient (see below).

Selecting the correct recipient with that name

If you have more than one recipient with the same name in your Address Book (or two addresses for the same person), you need to make absolutely certain that you're sending the e-mail to the correct address. Rather than type the recipient's name and have Outlook Express offer you the wrong recipient, follow this procedure:

1. In the **New Message** window, click on the ▣ To: icon on the left of the recipient text window.
2. In the left-hand pane of the **Select Recipients** dialog box that opens, click on the correct recipient/address you want to send the e-mail to.
3. Click on **To:->**.
4. Click on **OK**, or press ⌨ Enter ↵ .

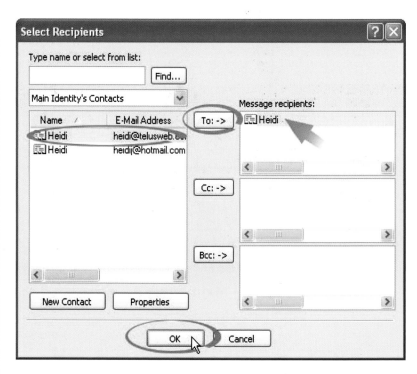

SENDING AN E-MAIL TO SEVERAL RECIPIENTS AT ONCE

 PROTECT THE PRIVACY OF PEOPLE'S E-MAIL ADDRESSES
People have a right to the privacy of their e-mail addresses. When sending the same letter to a number of people in one e-mail transmission it is therefore good practice not to allow the recipients to see the list of e-mail addresses to which you sent the e-mail.

TIP: MAKE SURE THE 'Bcc' WINDOW IS VISIBLE

For the next procedure, make sure that your new message shows the 📖 Bcc: button above the **Subject:** line. If not, in the Menu Bar click on **View**, then on **All Headers**.

It is not necessary to enter an address in the 📖 To: line when sending to multiple hidden recipients.

1. In your new message, enter the e-mail address of each recipient into the 📖 Bcc: window, separating each address by a comma and a space. (**Bcc** is short for **Blind carbon copy**, an old term to indicate that each recipient is unaware of who else received the letter.)
2. Type your message, and send the e-mail as usual.

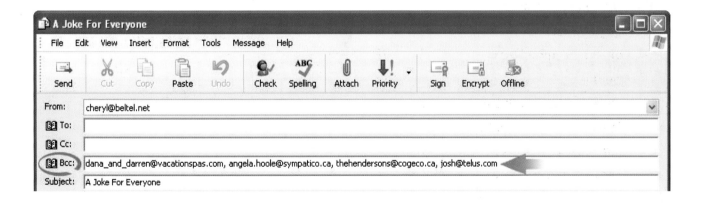

FINDING AN E-MAIL YOU'RE LOOKING FOR

1. In the **Folders** pane, click on the mail box in which you think the e-mail is stored.
2. Decide the criterion you think will be the easiest to help you find the e-mail (by sender, by subject or by date) and click on the applicable heading in the list pane on the right.
3. To change the sequence between ascending and descending order simply click again on the same heading.
4. If you can't find the e-mail by using one heading, try clicking on another.

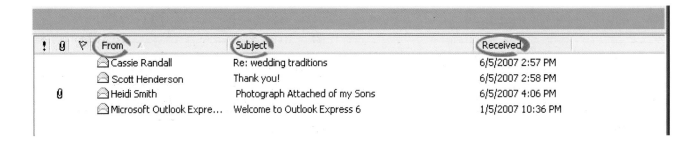

In Book 2 you'll learn some additional useful features of Outlook Express. You'll also learn how easy it is to communicate online with family, friends and colleagues in *real time* using the easy instant messaging program called Windows Messenger that comes bundled with Windows XP.

With Messenger both parties can respond to each other there and then in a live 'text chat' session, even live voice chat. So there's lots of fun still to be had with your Internet communications!

CONCLUSION

We hope you've enjoyed working your way through this beginner's manual with us and discovering that using a computer is not so difficult after all.

Computer Book 2 will take you further along the road to becoming an accomplished computer user. You'll learn how to get more out of your Internet and e-mail experiences. Book 2 also covers some very important things every computer user should know – such as how to keep your computer running efficiently, basic problem solving and folder management. And you'll get to know about some of the other useful applications and *help* systems that are part of Windows XP.

All the best!

6 Quick reference

We suggest you visit our Web site every now and then to find out what's new. And remember, if you have a specific question you'd like an answer to, try the Discussion Forum at our Web site: **www.reallyeasycomputerbooks.com**

USEFUL SHORTCUTS

DOCUMENTS AND FILES		MOVE CURSOR	
Go to a specific page	Ctrl + G	To end of line	End
Open a document	Ctrl + O	To beginning of line	Hom
Start a new document	Ctrl + N	To end of document	Ctrl + End
Print	F7 + P	To beginning of document	Ctrl + Hom
Save	Ctrl + S		
HELP		**TEXT ALIGNMENT**	
Help	Ctrl + F1	Left	Ctrl + L
Find	Ctrl + F	Right	Ctrl + R
Spelling check	F7	Centred	Ctrl + E
		Justified	Ctrl + J
FONT FORMATTING		**SELECTING TEXT**	
Bold	Ctrl + B	Select line	Click in margin
Underline	Ctrl + U	Select paragraph	Double-click in margin
Italics	Ctrl + I	Select all	Ctrl + A
COPY, CUT, PASTE			
Copy to Clipboard	Ctrl + C		
Cut to Clipboard	Ctrl + X		
Paste here	Ctrl + V		

IMPORTANT E-MAIL ADDRESSES

Name	E-mail address
....	....
....	....
....	....
....	....
....	....
....	....
....	....
....	....
....	....
....	....

IMPORTANT INTERNET WEB SITES

Name	Web site address – http://www.
....	....
....	....
....	....
....	....
....	....
....	....
....	....
....	....
....	....
....	....

MY LOG-IN DETAILS

For (e.g. Internet, e-mail)	User name	Password
....	....	....
....	....	....
....	....	....
....	....	....
....	....	....
....	....	....
....	....	....
....	....	....
....	....	....

Index

A

address book 85–88
  add sender to 85
  adding addresses 86–87
  using when creating new
    e-mail 88
addresses, e-mail 86
address window
    (Internet Explorer) 61, 62
advanced search tips
    (Internet) 69
ADSL 55
aligning text 48
attached files, viewing 81–82
attachments – viruses and security
    risks 82
attachments, large 76
attaching files to e-mail 75–76

B

Bcc (Blind Carbon Copy) 89
bold typing 39
bookmarking Web sites 65
booting up 7
bullets icon 50
bullets 50–51

C

capital letters 28
Capslock key 28
centring text 48
choosing an ISP 55
clicking (mouse) 9
closing (exiting) a file 31–32
closing a program 15
colour, changing the font 40
computer set-up 4
connecting

to mail server 71
to the Internet 57–59, 60
copying and moving text 45–46
creating a typed document 19

D

default 40
deleting e-mails 83
deleted e-mails, retrieving 83
Desktop 8, 56
dial-up 61
dial-up connection 58
disc scan 16
disconnecting
  from e-mail 79
  from the Internet 59, 79
document (see also file)
  attaching to e-mail 75–76
  closing 31–32
  moving to different places in 44–45
  opening a saved 33
  printing 34–35
  saving a Word 24–26
  starting a new 31
  typing 27

E

e-mail 71
  access requirements 71
  adding addresses to address book
    85, 86–87
  add sender to address
    book 85
  addresses, privacy 89
  attaching a file to 75, 76
  connecting 74
  deleting 83
  deleting in error 83

disconnecting from Internet 79
  finding specific 90
  forwarding 85
  Inbox 79–80
  managing 90
  manual addressing 86
  multiple recipients 89
  new mail 73, 79
  opening Outlook Express 72
  Outbox 77, 78
  previewing 80
  reading 79, 80
  receiving 78, 79
  retrieving deleted 83
  reply all 85
  reply to sender 84
  saving an address 85, 86–87
  send and receive 77, 78
  sending 77–78
  sending to several recipients 89
  Sent Items mail box 78
  setting up account 71
  setting up e-mail settings 56
  test 74
  using address book 88
  viewing attached files 81, 82
  viruses and security risks 82
  writing e-mail 72–75
Enter key 29, 36
exiting a program 15
Explorer (Internet Explorer) 61

F

Favorites (Internet) 65–66
favourite Web sites 65
file (see also document)
  closing 31–32
  creating 27

opening saved 33

printing 34–35

saving 26

starting a new 31

filling the whole screen 13

Firewall 57–58

font, changing the 37–41

formatting toolbar 37

forwarding e-mail 85

G

Google (search engine) 67

H

highlighting (selecting) text 42

home pages (Web sites) 64, 66

I

inactive window 22

Inbox 79–80

inserting page numbers 51

Internet 53, 60

  access requirements 54

  connection 57

  disconnecting from 59, 79

  going to a specific Web site 62–63

  high-speed connection 55

  Internet Explorer 61

  Internet Explorer address

    window 61

  narrowing down a search 69

  navigating Web pages 63

  protecting your computer 57

  remembering (bookmarking) a

    specific Web site (Favorites)

    65–66

  router 55

  searching for information 62, 67

  security, personal 70

  setting up 56

  surfing 60

package 55

italic typing 39

ISP (Internet Service Provider) 53

ISP, choosing an 55

ISP, getting help from 59

J

justification 48

K

keyboard 27

L

large attachments 76

lining up (aligning) text 48

loading a program 9–11

log in 7

logging off/on 17–18

M

mail (see also e-mail)

  deleting 83

  forwarding 85

  reading 79–80

  sending 77–78

  sending to several recipients 89

  writing 72–75

manually addressing (e-mail) 86

maximizing a window 13

menu bar 22, 32

menu, Start 10

menus, shortened 23

Microsoft Word 11, 22–23

  aligning paragraphs 48–49

  aligning text 48

  automatic page numbering 51–52

  changing the font 41

  copying text 46

  cutting text 47

  displaying toolbars 37

  document layout views 30

  font colour 40

  formatting paragraphs 49

  formatting toolbar 38

  indenting 30

  italics 39

  itemised lists 50

  justifying text 48

  layout views 30

  multiple font formats 41

  new document 31

  pasting copied text 46–47

  selecting entire document 43

  shortcuts to select text 42

  tab key 30

  typing in bold 39

  underlining 39

  window 21

minimizing a window 14

mouse, middle button or wheel 9

mouse pad 4

moving around a document 44

moving text 45

MS Word 19

N

name, user 7

narrowing down an Internet

  search 69

navigating Web pages 62, 63

new contact 86–87

new e-mail 73, 88

numbering, page 51

numbers, inserting 50–51

O

opening (starting) a new

  document 31

opening (loading) a program 9–11

opening a saved document or file 33

opening Internet Explorer 61

Outbox 77, 78

Outlook Express 71, 72

operating system 8

P

package, Internet 55

page down key 45

page numbers, inserting 51

page up key 45

password 7

pasting text 46–47

personal Internet security 70

power-on/off button 6

previewing e-mail 80

print icon 35

printing a document or file
    34–35

program, closing (exiting) 15

privacy, e-mail addresses 89

Q

quick reference 91

R

reading (viewing) attached files 81–82

receiving e-mail 78–79

reading e-mail 79–80

recipients (e-mail), multiple 89

reference, quick 91

remembering (bookmarking) a Web
    site 65–66

replying to an e-mail 84

reply all 85

retrieving deleted e-mail 83

Return (Enter) key 29, 36

requirements, Internet access 54

requirements, e-mail access 54

restarting (rebooting) 17

S

saving a Word document or file
    24–26

scan, disc, when computer is not shut
    down correctly 16

screen
    filling (maximizing) 13
    minimizing 14
    Welcome 7

search engines (Internet) 67, 69

search (Internet), narrowing down 69

search tips (Internet), advanced 69

security, personal (Internet) 70

security risks and viruses in
    e-mail attachments 82

selecting (highlighting) text 42

send and receive e-mails 77, 78

sending e-mail 77
    to several recipients 89

sent items 78

setting up e-mail 71

setting up e-mail settings 56

Shift key 28

shortcut, dial-up 56

shortcuts, cutting, copying and
    pasting 47

shortened menus 23

shutting down a computer 16

shutting down a program 15

Start button 8, 10

Start menu 10

surfing (navigating) the
    Internet 63

switching on 6

switch user 18

T

taskbar 14

testing e-mail 74

text
    aligning 48
    copying 45, 46
    highlighting (selecting) 42
    moving 45

pasting 46, 47

toggling 14

tower 6

typing 27
    bold 39
    capital letters 29
    colour 40
    italics 39
    underlining 39

turning off (shutting down)
    16, 17

U

underlining text 39

user, switch 18

user name 7

URL 62

V

view entire page 13

viruses and security risks in
    e-mail attachments 82

W

Web, searching for information on
    62, 67

Web sites, favourites 65

Web sites, home pages 66

Web site
    bookmarking (favourites) 65
    going to a specific 62–63
    searching for information 62, 67
    World Wide Web (www) 60

Web pages, navigating 62, 63

welcome screen 7

WordPad 11

writing (typing) a document or file 27

writing e-mail 72–74

This edition published in 2007 by New Holland Publishers (UK) Ltd
London · Cape Town · Sydney · Auckland
Garfield House, 86-88 Edgware Road, London W2 2EA, United Kingdom
80 McKenzie Street, Cape Town 8001, South Africa
Level 1, Unit 4, 14 Aquatic Drive, Frenchs Forrest, NSW 2086, Australia
218 Lake Road, Northcote, Auckland, New Zealand

First published in 2007 by
Struik Publishers
(a division of New Holland Publishing (South Africa) (Pty) Ltd)

www.newhollandpublishers.com

2 4 6 8 10 9 7 5 3

Publishing Manager: Linda de Villiers
Editor: Gavin Barfield
Designer: Janine Damon
Illustrator: Cheryl Smith
Proofreader and Indexer: Irma van Wyk
Series concept: Gavin Hoole

Reproduction by Hirt & Carter Cape (Pty) Ltd
Printed and bound by Craft Print International Ltd, Singapore

ISBN 978 1 84537 791 5